...hed
...nds,
...avel.

...s our
...crets
...orld,
...th of
...avel.

**Rely on Thomas Cook as your
travelling companion on your next trip
and benefit from our unique heritage.**

Thomas Cook **pocket** guides

MEXICO
CANCÚN & THE RIVIERA MAYA

Thom

Written by Jane Egginton and Iain MacIntyre, updated by Caroline Lascom

Published by Thomas Cook Publishing
A division of Thomas Cook Tour Operations Limited.
Company registration no. 3772199 England
The Thomas Cook Business Park, Unit 9, Coningsby Road,
Peterborough PE3 8SB, United Kingdom
Email: books@thomascook.com, Tel: + 44 (0) 1733 416477
www.thomascookpublishing.com

Produced by Cambridge Publishing Management Limited
Burr Elm Court, Main Street, Caldecote CB23 7NU

ISBN: 978-1-84848-267-8

© 2006, 2008 Thomas Cook Publishing
This third edition © 2010
Text © Thomas Cook Publishing
Maps © Thomas Cook Publishing/PCGraphics (UK) Limited

Series Editor: Adam Royal
Production/DTP: Steven Collins

Printed and bound in Spain by GraphyCems

Front cover photography © Thomas Cook

CONTENTS

WHAT'S IN YOUR GUIDEBOOK?

Independent authors Impartial, up-to-date information from our travel experts who meticulously source local knowledge.

Experience Thomas Cook's 165 years in the travel industry and guidebook publishing enriches every word with expertise you can trust.

Travel know-how Thomas Cook has thousands of staff working around the globe, all living and breathing travel.

Editors Travel-publishing professionals, pulling everything together to craft a perfect blend of words, pictures, maps and design.

You, the traveller We deliver a practical, no-nonsense approach to information, geared to how you really use it.

● *Mexico is a colourful and diverse country*

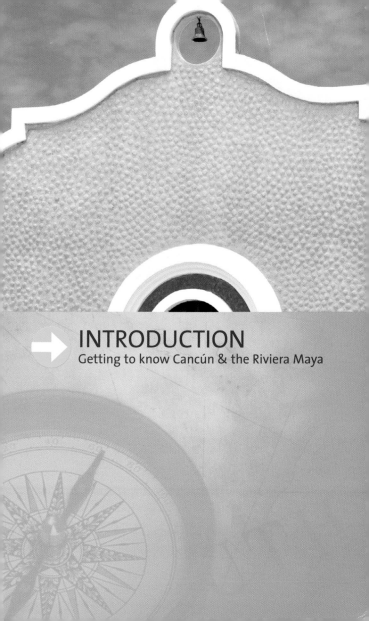

INTRODUCTION
Getting to know Cancún & the Riviera Maya

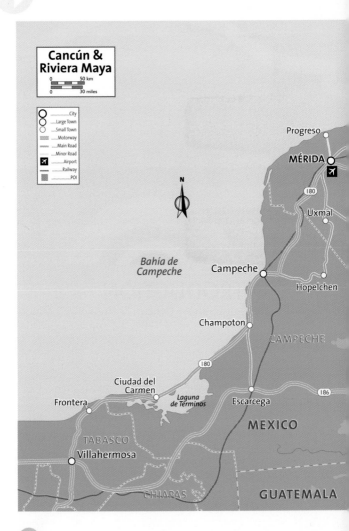

Cancún &
Riviera Maya

| | 0 | 50 km |
| 0 | 30 miles |

○	City
○	Large Town
○	Small Town
	Motorway
	Main Road
	Minor Road
✈	Airport
	Railway
	POI

N

Progreso

MÉRIDA ✈

180

Uxmal

Bahía de
Campeche

Campeche

Hopelchen

CAMPECHE

Champoton

180

Ciudad del
Carmen

Laguna
de Terminos

Escarcega

186

Frontera

MEXICO

TABASCO

Villahermosa

CHIAPAS

GUATEMALA

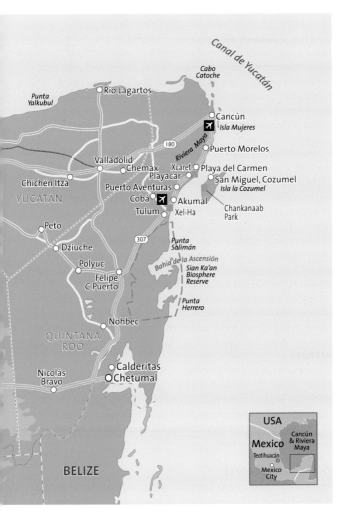

Getting to know Cancún & the Riviera Maya

Mexico conjures up images of cowboys and Indians, deserts and cacti, tequila and tropical jungle. As a holiday destination, it is exotic yet friendly, with a sunny climate and delicious food. The country has world-class beaches, a rich culture and great shopping. Well established as a tourist destination, its resorts are sophisticated, while much of the countryside is unspoilt.

Mexico is sandwiched between the southern states of the USA and the Central American countries of Guatemala and Belize. It is flanked by the huge sweep of the Gulf of Mexico and the Caribbean Sea to the east and the Pacific Ocean on its western side. Cancún and the Riviera Maya form a strip on the eastern coast of the Yucatán Peninsula – a large tongue of land on the Caribbean coast of Mexico. The area's high concentration of spectacular beaches and Mayan sites makes it extremely popular. Cancún is without doubt the holidaymakers' mecca, but the long string of much smaller and quieter resorts stretching south (known as the Riviera Maya) are gaining in popularity.

Spanish is spoken throughout the country, although many people are unaware that more than 50 native Indian languages are also in use. In tourist areas, English is widely spoken, but a little Spanish goes a long way.

HISTORY

This is a land rich in history, well known for its archaeological remains and its folk art. The Spanish first arrived in Mexico on Isla Mujeres in 1517 (see page 25). In the space of a few short and brutal years, they conquered the entire country, and held onto it for three centuries. As a result, 60 per cent of today's population is a mix of Spanish and Indian descent, known as *mestizo*.

THE MEXICAN PEOPLE

The people of Mexico – over 100 million strong, with one fifth crammed in around Mexico City – are as diverse as the country's destinations, and

Indians, descendants of Mexico's pre-Hispanic inhabitants, have retained much of their culture and language. The country is deeply religious – around 90 per cent of Mexicans are Roman Catholic, and most villages host annual festivals in honour of their local patron saint. Mexico's street life is colourful, with the *zócalo* (main square) its focus. Enjoying a rich tradition of feasting and festivals, Mexicans know how to enjoy life and even celebrate death during 'the Day of the Dead' (see 'Festivals & events', page 106). Many people live in vibrant, modern cities, but scattered along the coast are several unspoilt fishing villages, and inland are mountain settlements where life has changed little in the last hundred years.

🔺 *Man dressed in typical costume from western Mexico*

THE BEST OF CANCÚN & THE RIVIERA MAYA

From glistening white sand beaches and ethereal jungles to mystical archaeological sites and colonial cities, the Riviera Maya is not surprisingly hailed as a tropical paradise.

TOP 10 ATTRACTIONS

- **Playa del Carmen** With turquoise waters, sweeping sands, watersports galore and a fun, party atmosphere, Playa strikes the perfect balance between relaxation and adventure (see page 40).

- **Puerto Morelos** Escape the big, brash resorts and snorkel among manta rays and turtles, then lie back on a pristine virgin beach, cocktail in hand (see page 34).

- **Bottlenose dolphins** The waters of the Riviera Maya are a fertile breeding ground for these awe-inspiring creatures, which are best seen in their natural habitat (see page 19).

- **The Day of the Dead** This is a jubilant and surreal festival at the beginning of November, when Mexicans prepare for the spirits of their loved ones to visit them from the other side (see page 106).

- **The Feast of the Virgin de Guadalupe** A kaleidoscopic outburst of national expression, with feasting, fireworks, music and dance (see page 106).

- **Cobá** Barely excavated temples rise above the jungle canopy, evoking the architectural genius of the Maya (see page 74).

- **Chichén Itzá** The largest archaeological site in the region is centred upon the sublime El Castillo, upon whose steps the sun's rays project the shadow of a writhing serpent during the spring and autumn equinoxes (see page 72).

- **Valladolid** Get under the skin of the real Mexico with a visit to this charming city with its glorious colonial buildings (see page 84).

- **Sian Ka'an Biosphere** Rainforest, savanna and wetlands form this wildlife reserve, with a rich biodiversity that includes more than 330 bird species, howler monkeys and jaguars (see page 80).

- **Scuba diving** Mexico's Yucatán offers some of the best scuba diving in the world, especially off the island of Cozumel (see page 60).

◗ *Mayan ruins at Tulum*

SYMBOLS KEY
The following symbols are used throughout this book:

ⓐ address ⓣ telephone ⓦ website address ⓔ email
ⓛ opening times ⓘ important

The following symbols are used on the maps:

🇮 information office		○	city
✉ post office		○	large town
▣ shopping		○	small town
✈ airport		■	POI (point of interest)
✚ hospital		▬	motorway
Ⓥ police station		—	main road
▤ bus station		—	minor road
▤ railway station		—	railway
✝ church		Ⓜ	metro

❶ numbers denote featured cafés, restaurants & evening venues

RESTAURANT CATEGORIES
The symbol after the name of each restaurant listed in this guide
indicates the price of a typical three-course meal without drinks
for one person:
£ under £12   ££ £12–45   £££ more than £45

▶ *The region offers fabulous beaches and plenty of sunshine*

RESORTS
Places under the sun

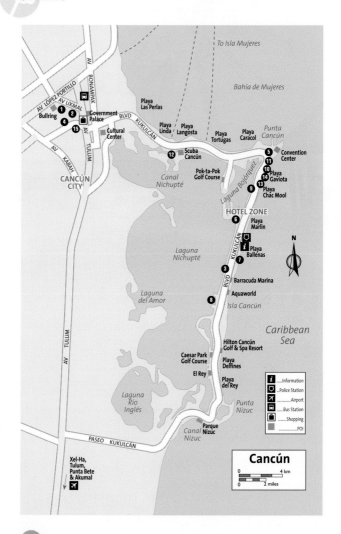

Cancún

The story goes that in 1967 Mexican tourist officials were looking to build a new resort and their computer came up with Cancún as the perfect location. At the time, it was nothing but an offshore sand barrier, home to 100 Mayan fishermen. Two causeways were built to connect it to the mainland, and hotel after hotel sprung up along the 24-km (15-mile) beach, sandwiched between the sheltered lagoon and the Caribbean Sea. With year-round sun, safe swimming, watersports, fishing, golf and plenty of hotels, beach bars, shops and restaurants, it's no wonder this has become Mexico's most popular resort – just as the computer predicted.

Cancún sits on the east coast of the Yucatán Peninsula, in the state of Quintana Roo. Just offshore is the longest coral reef in the Americas, stretching for 500 km (310 miles) along the coast. The Yucatán's major international airport is located here, as are consulates, doctors, major car rental companies and many other services. Cancún itself is divided into two areas: the **Hotel Zone** around the lagoon; and **Cancún City** (also known simply as 'downtown'), which started as a village for the workers in the tourism industry. The downtown area offers visitors a change from the beachfront Hotel Zone, with bustling markets, buzzing bars where *mariachi* bands play, and some great restaurants and shops. Prices are also a bit lower and the ambience is more genuinely Latin.

BEACHES

The peninsular Hotel Zone is one long beach, with the lagoon on one side, and most hotels fronting the ocean on the other. The ocean side is the place to go for swimming and tanning, while jet-skis, kayaks and other rentals are on the lagoon side. One of the best things about Cancún is that the sand is crushed coral rather than crushed rock, so it stays cool underfoot even on the hottest days.

The flat, sandy seabeds and shallow waters of **Playa Caracol** and **Punta Cancún**, at the northern end of the Hotel Zone, are perfect for children. **Playa Langosta**, **Playa Las Perlas** and **Playa Tortugas** feature all kinds of beach games and diving and snorkelling tours, as well as regular shuttles to the island retreat of **Isla Mujeres** (see page 25). And, of course, there are plenty of bars and restaurants.

The beaches on the east coast benefit from the ocean breeze, but have bigger waves. **Playa Ballenas** is a great place to people-watch, and tube rides, volleyball and parasailing will keep you amused. The views from **Playa Delfines** and **Punta Nizuc** are fantastic, and the latter is home to some of the more upmarket hotels.

Right at the northern tip of the Hotel Zone is a gem of a beach that can only be accessed by walking through the property of the **Camino Real Hotel** at Punta Cancún. (The beach itself is public property, as are all beaches in Mexico, so don't be put off choosing your favourite in the Hotel Zone, even if it looks private.) There are no hawkers, no music and no volleyball, which can be a welcome change.

● *Tulum's cliff-top location has excellent sea views*

South of Cancún, the beaches of **Punta Bete** (58 km/36 miles) and **Akumal** (100 km/60 miles) are both spectacular. Akumal in particular is renowned for its good snorkelling and diving (see page 65).

THINGS TO SEE & DO

Archaeology

Towards the south end of the Hotel Zone are the ruins of **El Rey** (The King). Inhabited from the 10th century AD until the beginning of the 16th century, its structures include plazas surrounded by buildings and several platforms that are connected by a long pathway. The site takes its name from a skeleton uncovered there, which was thought to possibly be a former Mayan king. The archaeological museum in the Hotel Zone's Convention Center exhibits jewels, masks, skulls and other artefacts from the postclassic period.

ⓐ Boulevard Kukulcán Km 19 ⓣ 998 883 0305

Game fishing

Cancún is a fishing paradise with barracuda, sailfish, marlin and tuna all on offer. To stand a good chance of catching big fish like marlin or sailfish, it's best to take an eight-hour charter at least.

Aquaworld offers tours. ⓐ Boulevard Kukulcán Km 15.2 ⓣ 998 848 8327

Cancún Vista offers all-day trips, night fishing and deep-sea tours.

ⓐ Avenida Coba 31, Edificio Monaco, Oficina 2 ⓣ 998 887 8069

ⓦ www.cancunvista.com

Golf

The **Hilton Cancún Golf & Spa Resort** offers an immaculately kept, 18-hole, par 72 golf course, with a practice tee and putting green. At the time of writing, green fees were around US$200 for non-Hilton guests, including the golf cart fee.

ⓐ Boulevard Kukulcán Km 17 ⓣ 998 881 8000

ⓦ www.hiltoncancun.com/golf

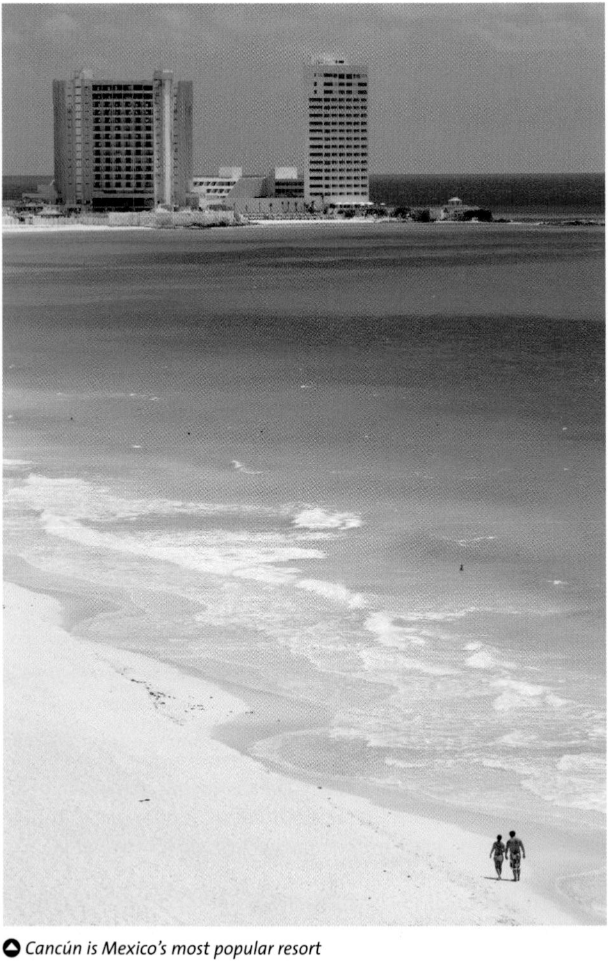

Cancún is Mexico's most popular resort

Snorkelling & diving

The waters around Cancún offer amazing opportunities for experienced divers, but, with visibility in the water of up to 76 m (250 ft), even amateurs will have fun snorkelling. The best area off the beach is near the Westin Regina, in the southern tip of the Hotel Zone. For most of the other places (Isla Mujeres, Cozumel or some of the lagoons) you will need to sign up for a tour, or it is an easy ferry ride for the more independent of spirits.

Barracuda Marina ⓐ Boulevard Kukulcán Km 14 ❶ 998 885 3444 , or **Scuba Cancún** ⓐ Boulevard Kukulcán Km 5 ❶ 998 849 7508 ⓦ www.scubacancun.com.mx

Swimming with dolphins

At the southern tip of the Hotel Zone is Parque Nizuc, home to the **Wet'n Wild Water Park** (see page 102) and the ocean-fronted **Atlantida**, where you can learn all about bottlenose dolphins and then take a 30-minute swim with them in a sea enclosure. Cost is included in entry to the main park.

ⓐ Boulevard Kukulcán Km 25 ❶ 998 881 3000

EXCURSIONS
Chichén Itzá

Don't miss the chance to visit this ancient Mayan city (see page 72). Most organised tours to Chichén Itzá depart around 08.00, and it is a three-hour trip to the site. Tours are advertised at most hotels, or you can book over the internet (ⓦ www.chichen-itza-tour.com). There are cheap, comfortable hotels close to most of the main Mayan sites, so check in the night before if you want to avoid the crowds on your visit. Many sites open at 08.00, but the tour buses arrive at around 11.00.

Sian Ka'an Biosphere

This beautiful, vast wildlife reserve (see page 80), which covers 528,000 hectares (nearly 1$\frac{1}{3}$ million acres), includes rainforest, mangroves, savannas and marine environments. The biodiversity here stretches from tiny, colourful butterflies to families of howler monkeys, crocodiles, jaguars and tapirs. Among the 330-plus bird species is the jabiru stork, the world's largest bird capable of flight. **EcoColors** offers a variety of tours (☎ 998 884 3667 ⓦ www.ecotravelmexico.com).

Tulum & Xel-Ha

From its cliff-top perch, the ancient settlement of **Tulum** (see page 78), 130 km (80 miles) south of Cancún, commands a terrific view of the

SHOPPING

Most shops in Cancún are open daily from 10.00 until about 20.00 or 22.00. Some smaller downtown shops will close for siesta, however, which is usually from 14.00 until around 17.00.

Kukulcán Plaza has hundreds of shops, including several selling designer clothing, as well as banks, theatres and upscale US franchise restaurants (⊜ Boulevard Kukulcán Km 13).

Downtown, you are more likely to find a bargain, and certainly more authentic shopping opportunities. **The Ki Huic Open Air Market** (⊜ Avenida Tulum) is the city's oldest crafts bazaar. Here you'll find goods such as leather, pewter, carved wood, pottery, hammocks, rugs, baskets, and traditional Mexican clothing items like *huaraches* (sandals) and *huipiles* (colourful, embroidered Mayan dresses).

La Isla Shopping Village is an open-air mall complete with winding canals and an aquarium (⊜ Boulevard Kukulcán Km 12.5 ⓦ www.laislacancun.com.mx).

For food shopping, casual clothing, shoes, beach towels and sunscreen, Cancún's downtown supermarkets are the cheapest option. Most open at 07.00 and close at 24.00, although **Walmart** is open 24 hours a day. To get there from the Hotel Zone take the bus Ruta No 15 and ask the driver to drop you off at the Walmart bus stop.

Caribbean Sea. The largest building, El Castillo, may at one time have served as a lighthouse. Between this and the 'Temple of the Wind', a break in the steep cliff gives way to a beautiful beach of fine sand. The easy access to the sea supports the view that Tulum was a departure point for fishing and trading vessels and one of the main ports of the Mayan civilisation.

Many of the tours leaving from Cancún are combined with a visit to nearby **Xel-Ha**, an 'eco' theme park (see page 83). This is a great spot for snorkelling, with thousands of brightly coloured tropical fish to see, and it's also a great place to relax.

TAKING A BREAK

You will never be short of dining options in Cancún. Every fast food outlet you can think of is here, as well as a host of fantastic restaurants serving good food in gorgeous settings. Prices in the Hotel Zone restaurants match the going rate in the USA, which means they are cheaper than the UK – downtown you will find some great bargains. However, while some of the cheapest and best restaurants are downtown, taxis from the Hotel Zone can be overpriced. Instead, catch the bus to the Chedarui supermarket – then hail a taxi to your restaurant of choice. Prices are very reasonable for both.

Labná £ ❶ Yucatán specialities are served against a backdrop of evocative photographs of the peninsula. A bewildering menu features chicken pibil, pocchuc and suckling pig. If you can't decide, try the Labná special, which provides sampler portions of four entrées.
ⓐ Avenida Margaritas 29 ❶ 998 892 3056
ⓦ www.labna.com/english ❶ 12.00–22.00 daily

La Parrilla £ ❷ Popular with tourists and locals, the food here is authentic and beautifully prepared, while the superb margaritas, daiquiris and live music will keep the conversation flowing. ⓐ Avenida Yaxchilán 51
❶ 998 884 5398 ⓦ www.laparrilla.com.mx ❶ 12.00–23.00 daily

La Dolce Vita ££ ③ A reasonably priced Italian favourite, with a fine selection of seafood and home-made pastas. From the restaurant, diners have a fine view of the lagoon and Cancún's spectacular sunsets.
ⓐ Boulevard Kukulcán Km 14.6, opposite the Marriott Hotel
ⓣ 998 885 0161 ⓛ 12.00–24.00 daily

La Habichuela ££ ④ Over the past 30 years, this unmissable downtown restaurant has built up a solid reputation for its fine Caribbean food and the magical ambience of its Mayan garden area.
ⓐ Avenida Margaritas 25, next to 'Las Palapas' Park ⓣ 998 884 3158
ⓦ www.lahabichuela.com ⓛ 12.00–24.00 daily

100% Natural ££ ⑤ This is a great place for a healthy breakfast or lunch. The shakes and smoothies here are legendary, and there are plenty of vegetarian takes on traditional Mexican food. The setting is magnificent with huge plants and trees dotted around the outdoor dining area. ⓐ Plaza Caracol (Hotel Zone) and Avenida Yaxchilán (downtown) ⓣ 998 884 3617 ⓛ 08.00–22.00 daily

Thai ££ ⑥ A truly memorable dining experience with individual *palapas* dotting the lushly arboreal lagoon. Relax with a signature cocktail while local DJ talent spins ambient tunes, before dining on spicy Thai specialities: the satay and pad thai are favourites among local and tourist diners. Reservations highly recommended. ⓐ Boulevard Kukulcán Km 12.5
ⓣ 998 176 8070 ⓛ 17.30–01.00 daily

Aioli £££ ⑦ A wonderful choice for a romantic evening, Aioli is widely considered one of the best – and most expensive – restaurants in Cancún. The gourmet French cuisine is without peer. Save room for the sublime desserts. ⓐ Le Méridien Resort, Retorno del Rey Km 14
ⓣ 998 881 2200 ⓛ 06.30–23.00 daily

Laguna Grill £££ ⑧ Exotic dishes are served in a captivating tropical garden that overlooks the lagoon. Fresh fish is given an Asian twist;

shrimp tempura and *ahi tuna ceviche* are a refreshing preamble to expertly prepared entrées, such as fillet with garlic mashed potato. Truly memorable event dining. ⓐ Boulevard Kukulcán Km 15.6 ⓣ 998 885 0267 ⓦ www.lagunagrill.com.mx ⓛ 14.00–24.00 daily

Lorenzillos £££ ⓽ Jutting out into the lagoon, this high-class restaurant specialises in live lobster. Carnivores can opt for the almond-encrusted fillet. ⓐ Boulevard Kukulcán Km 10.5 ⓣ 998 883 1234 ⓦ www.lorenzillos.com.mx ⓛ 13.00–00.30 daily ❶ Reservations necessary; smart dress advised

⬥ *Lorenzillos, Cancún*

AFTER DARK

Cancún lives to party. Most hotel bars spill out onto the beach and are open until late, and then the party really starts at the huge superclubs and bars that are spread throughout the Hotel Zone. American college students come here in droves during their 'spring break', from late February to the middle of March, when the clubs are at their busiest. Many of the hotels have deals with bars and clubs, and may offer you a wristband for free entry or discounted drinks. Cheap buses run the length of the hotel strip all night. Have small change ready, and just give the driver a nod when you want to get off.

You could do worse than start your evening with some cool drinks and reggae at the **Terrasta reggae bar** ❿ (ⓐ Boulevard Kukulcán Km 9.5 ❶ 998 883 3333). **Coco Bongo** ⓫ is large, loud and crowded and the dance music is interspersed with mini-shows and trapeze acts. Sizeable queues form after midnight (❶ 998 883 5061). With a capacity of 3,500, **La Boom** ⓬ is one of Cancún's biggest venues. All drinks are included in the admission price, but the waiters still expect to be tipped for prompt service. Sounds are rave, RnB and techno, with an adjacent hip-hop bar (❶ 998 849 7587). **Dady'O** ⓭ is among the best clubs in Cancún, with first-class sound and lighting technology and a spectacular 3D laser show. The club has five bars and a snack bar (ⓐ Boulevard Kukulcán Km 9.5 ❶ 998 883 3333). Next to the Dady'O nightclub is the **O Ultra Lounge** ⓭, part of the same franchise, but with a more laid-back atmosphere, fine cocktails and good DJ sets (ⓐ Boulevard Kukulcán Km 9.5).

If it's all about the music, then **The City** ⓮ is the place. Cancún's state-of-the-art club plays host to big-name DJs from around the world, and – if you can believe it – has capacity for beach parties of 15,000 (ⓦ www.thecitycancun.com).

For Latin music, **Mambo Café** ⓯ features live music and steamy dance routines including salsa, merengue and samba. Thursday is the most crowded night, when ladies drink free (ⓐ Plaza las Avenidas ❶ 998 840 6498 ⓦ www.mambocafe.com.mx).

Isla Mujeres

Only a short ferry ride from the towering hotels of Cancún, tiny Isla Mujeres is nonetheless a million miles away in atmosphere. Francisco Hernández de Córdoba, the first European to visit the Yucatán, gave the island its name – which means 'Island of Women' – when he came ashore in 1517 and found clay statuettes of partially clad women.

Although it has now been discovered by tourists, Isla Mujeres retains much of its sleepy, fishing village charm and is still cheaper than Cancún. It is only 8 km long and 2 km wide (5 x 1 ¼ miles), but the island is home to some fantastic beaches and fine restaurants. Its setting is tropical, with a sea that is turquoise blue and warm all year round. There are plenty of activities to keep the whole family amused, and the regular fast ferry to the mainland makes it a great base for exploring the Riviera Maya. There are good snorkelling areas, and some of the better swimming beaches are to the south along the western shore. The ferry docks, town and most popular beach, **Playa Cocoteros**, also known as **Playa Norte** and **Nautibeach**, are at the northern tip of the island. It's easy to find your way around the grid of narrow streets in the town, and there is a main plaza that also serves as a basketball court just inland from the ferry docks.

BEACHES

The sands on the west coast of the island are the most popular – despite the calm waters and good facilities, they are still uncrowded compared to Cancún. The windward side is even less developed, though the surf can sometimes be a little rough. **Playa Norte** is the most popular beach on the island and within easy reach of town. Kayaks, snorkelling gear, sunloungers and beach umbrellas can all be rented for a reasonable amount, and there are plenty of low-key beach bars where you can while away the hours with a cocktail under a thatched roof. **Playa Paraiso** and **Playa Lancheros** on the southwest coast of the island offer peaceful swimming in crystal-clear waters. **Playa Indios** is an exclusive beach famous for its shark pens.

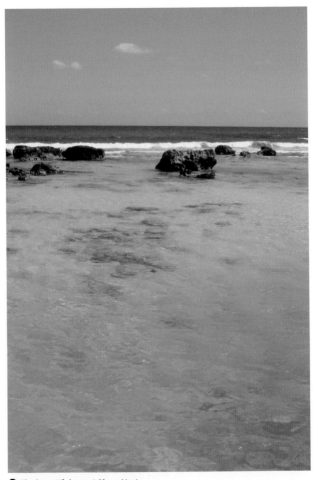

◆ *The beautiful sea at Playa Norte*

THINGS TO SEE & DO

El Garrafón Natural Reef Park

At the south end of the island, Garrafón is packed with quirky activities, both in the water and on land. You can explore underwater with 'Snuba' (similar to scuba diving, but with the air tanks on a floating raft above you) and 'Sea Trek', where a special helmet allows you to walk along the seabed. You can also hire snorkelling gear and glass-bottomed sea kayaks. On land, attractions include a zipline ride, observation tower, climbing pole, snack bars and restaurant. In the afternoon, the park becomes busy with Cancún day trippers.

ⓐ Garrafón-Punta Sur Km 6 ⓣ 998 849 4950 ⓦ www.garrafon.com

Hacienda Mundaca

Constructed by Fermín Mundaca, a notorious pirate and slave trader, the hacienda with its magnificent gardens was intended to house the unrequited love of his life, a local girl who preferred a younger man to the brutal, old corsair. Her rejection drove Mundaca slowly mad, and he died alone in distant Mérida, leaving behind his tomb in the Isla Mujeres cemetery, complete with engraved skull and crossbones. The hacienda and gardens have been restored and now a zoo has been added with snakes, birds, monkeys and the odd big cat.

ⓐ East of Avenida Rueda Medina, near Playa Lancheros

Laguna Maka

This mystical lagoon is believed to be the spot where bloodthirsty pirates lay in wait for Spanish vessels.

ⓐ Avenida Rueda Medina, around 3 km (2 miles) south of the town centre

Turtle Sanctuary

Always a hatching ground for the area's giant sea turtles – once killed for their meat and shells and their eggs dug up for food – the sanctuary is now a haven for these creatures that continue to lay their eggs in the soft sand here from May to September. The turtles are now under government protection and their eggs are placed in pens to keep them safe – hatchlings are then placed in tanks until they are large enough to be released into the wild. A visit here is an uplifting experience.

ⓐ Carretera Sac-Bajo, Laguna Makax ⓣ 998 877 0595 ⓛ 09.00–17.00 daily

EXCURSIONS
Birdwatching

North of Isla Mujeres, the tiny island of **Isla Contoy** is around 8 km (5 miles) long and is barely 20 m (22 yds) across at its widest point. Home to more than 70 bird species, including brown pelicans, roseate spoonbills, herons, kingfishers and cormorants, it also sees flocks of flamingos arrive in April. The best months to spot turtles burying their eggs in the sand at night are June, July and August. The island can be reached by a 45-minute boat trip from Isla Mujeres, but visitor numbers are restricted, so advance booking is recommended. Contact **Contoy Express Tours** (ⓣ 998 877 1367) for details of tours. Further afield is the **Sian Ka'an Biosphere** on the mainland (see page 80), a huge nature reserve where more than 330 bird species have been counted.

Mayan ruins

Although the remains of a temple to the Mayan goddess Ixchal can be found on the south tip of the island, the cliff-top ruins have suffered hurricane damage, and the main draw here is now the view. On the mainland coast, the ancient Mayan settlement of **Tulum** is soaked in history (see page 78). It's also possible to visit the spectacular ruins of the Mayan city of **Chichén Itzá** (see page 72) in one day, although overnight tours are also possible. Contact **Viajes Prisma** (ⓐ Avenida Rueda Medina 9C ⓣ 998 877 0938) for tour details.

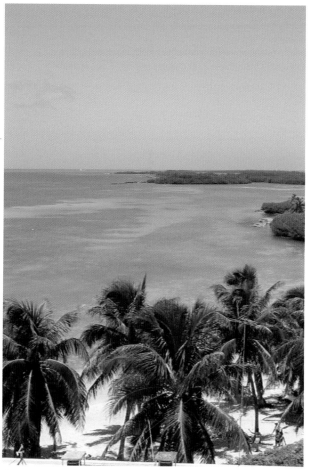

⬤ *Isla Contoy – Cancún's hidden gem*

TAKING A BREAK

Cafe Cito £ One of the best breakfast spots on the island, serving waffles, pancakes and omelettes cooked to order. Great cappuccinos.
ⓐ Avenida Matamoros 42 ❶ 998 877 1470 ❶ 08.00–23.00 daily

⬧ *Sailing at sunset off Isla Mujeres*

Elements of the island £ Trendy coffee house specialising in fresh juices and healthy breakfasts. ⓐ Avenida Benito Juárez 64, between López Mateos and Matamoros ⓣ 998 877 0736 ⓦ www.elementsoftheisland.com ⓛ 08.00–13.00 daily

Le Bistro Français ££ Colourful bistro-café serving French staples: coq au vin, filet mignon, seafood drenched with white wine and garlic, and delicious desserts. Charmingly rustic ambience and gracious owners. Also serves bountiful breakfasts. ⓐ Avenida Matamoros 29 ⓛ 08.00–12.00 & 18.00–22.00 Sun–Fri, 18.00–22.00 Sat

Casa O's ££ With its thatched roof and open sides it might look like a basic *palapa*, but a varied wine list, delicious seafood and friendly staff make this a contender for the best restaurant on the island. The lobster bisque is a must. ⓐ Calle Garrafón ⓣ 998 888 0170 ⓦ www.casaos.com ⓛ 13.00–23.00 daily

Mañana ££ A colourful, unpretentious spot focusing on Mediterranean flavours and healthy smoothies. An excellent lunch choice and plenty of vegetarian dishes are on offer. ⓐ Avenida Matamoros and Guerrero ⓣ 998 877 0555 ⓛ 08.00–22.00 Tues–Sat, closed Sun & Mon

Zahil Ha ££ Delicious Mexican fare combined with pasta and seafood in a beachside haven that is part of the Na Balam beach complex. ⓐ Calle Zazil-Ha 118, Playa Norte ⓣ 998 877 0279 ⓦ www.nabalam.com ⓛ 18.00–23.00 daily

Casa Rolandi £££ Part of the Villa Rolandi hotel complex, this restaurant serves fine international cuisine in a lovely location overlooking the Caribbean. ⓐ Carretera Sac-Bajo ⓣ 998 877 0700 ⓦ www.villarolandi.com ⓛ 08.00–23.00 daily

⬣ Bring home a Mexican tradition in the form of a colourful hammock

AFTER DARK

You won't be kept awake by endless loud music on Isla Mujeres. What you will find are pleasant bistros, laid-back beach bars and low-key venues playing good music in a friendly atmosphere. **Playa Sol** is the best beach bar for a sunset cocktail and live music (🅐 Playa Norte). Also on Playa Norte, the hotel bar at **Na Balam** draws a crowd until midnight with a happy hour from 17.00 until 20.00 and there is live music at weekends. At **Bar Om** you can pour your own draught beer at your table and listen to jazz, reggae and Latin music (🅐 Calle Matamoros). **La Peña**, with a roof terrace overlooking the sea, draws a relaxed, late-night crowd for dancing and playing pool (🅐 Avenida Guerrero, opposite Church Square). For a fine Margarita after midnight, head to **La Adelita**, where more than 100 varieties of tequila are on sale (🅐 Avenida Hidalgo 12A). **Las Palapas Chimbos** is a beachfront restaurant that has live music every night after 21.00.

SHOPPING

Isla Mujeres has most of the same choice of handicrafts, clothes and jewellery that you see in the mainland tourist shops, but they are often cheaper. You will find the usual branded T-shirts, but without the word 'Cancún', 'Cozumel' or even 'Isla Mujeres' splashed all over them. Many of the tourist shops are around the ferry dock area, and there is a supermarket at the east end of town. Visit **Artesanías Arco Iris** (🅐 Avenida Hidalgo and Juárez) for silver, stones and handicrafts such as blankets with intricate designs. **De Corazón** (🅐 Avenida Abasolo, between Hidalgo and Guerrero) is a small boutique stocking locally made cosmetics, jewellery, scented candles and crochet goods. For snorkelling or dive equipment try the **Bahía Dive Shop** (🅐 Avenida Rueda Medina 166) and for fine Cuban cigars try **Tobacco & Co** (🅐 Avenida Hidalgo 14, Plaza Rocateliz). Isla Mujeres is well known for its excellent-value gems. You can purchase stones loose and even in the rough. Try **Rachet & Rose** (🅐 Avenida Morelos, and Juárez).

Puerto Morelos

This quiet and peaceful village, well away from the main road, is frequently compared to the Playa del Carmen of 25 years ago. The locals still make a living from the sea, and visitors can enjoy a genuine Mexican experience at prices that put nearby Cancún to shame. Puerto Morelos is a perfect place for a relaxing beach holiday, and its location – halfway between Cancún and Playa del Carmen – means you can sample some great nightlife – but only if you feel like it.

The community, a mix of locals and foreigners, works hard to protect Puerto's status as a national marine park and keep development to a minimum. The focus of the village is the *zócalo* (main square), where you will find a handful of shops, bars, restaurants and a dive shop. A few steps away is an unspoilt, natural beach next to a small pier where fishermen bring ashore their daily catch for the village restaurants. From the pier, you can expect to be offered excursions to the reefs.

BEACHES

Just offshore is a shallow coral reef (now a national park). As a result, the seabed close to the shore features a lot of seagrass. Nonetheless, the water is crystal clear and the reef makes for some great snorkelling just a stone's throw from the beach.

The main beach, which is larger than it once was following the hurricanes of 2005, is right behind the *zócalo* (main square), and there are others to the south and north of the village. None of these is raked – except where hotel and restaurant owners choose to – but the beaches are clean, and devoid of the crowds and litter you might see elsewhere.

THINGS TO SEE & DO

Crocodile zoo

Just north of the village is **Croco Cun**, a zoological park that raises crocodiles and is home to monkeys, parrots, deer and other wildlife.

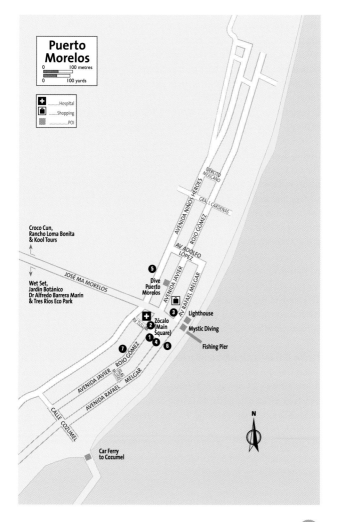

Puerto
Morelos

| 0 | 100 metres |
| 0 | 100 yards |

Hospital
Shopping
POI

Croco Cun,
Rancho Loma Bonita
& Kool Tours

JOSÉ MA MORELOS

Wet Set,
Jardín Botánico
Dr Alfredo Barrera Marín
& Tres Ríos Eco Park

EJERCITO
MEXICANO

GRAL L CARDENAS

AVENIDA NIÑOS HÉROES

ROJO GÓMEZ

AV ADOLFO
LOPEZ

AVENIDA JAVIER

AV RAFAEL MELGAR

5
Dive
Puerto
Morelos

3 Lighthouse

Zócalo
(Main
Square)

2

1

4 **6**

7

AV TULUM

ROJO GÓMEZ

ISIDRO
MUÑOZ

MELGAR

AVENIDA JAVIER

AVENIDA RAFAEL MELGAR

CALLE COZUMEL

Mystic Diving

Fishing Pier

Car Ferry
to Cozumel

N

The biologists who run the park have collected specimens of many of the reptiles that are indigenous to the area. An informative guided tour, which includes a visit to the reptile house and a sometimes hair-raising walk through the jungle (look out for the snakes, tarantulas and wild pigs), lasts 90 minutes. You may even get to handle a baby crocodile. There is a restaurant on site.

ⓐ Carretera 307 Km 31 ❶ 998 850 3719 Ⓦ www.crococunzoo.com ❶ 08.30–17.30 daily ❶ Make sure you wear insect repellent

Diving & snorkelling

The coral reef directly offshore is shallow – only 3 m (10 ft) at its deepest point, and snorkellers must wear a life jacket in order to remain near the surface and avoid damaging it. Visual delights include iridescent darting fish, eels, rays and even the odd turtle. Puerto Morelos really is a mecca for divers, with fantastic *cenote* (natural wells) dives, wall, wreck and open-water excursions to amuse beginners and experts alike.

Victor Reyes at **Mystic Diving** (❶ 998 871 0634) takes small groups out on tank dives and is a qualified PADI and NAUI instructor. Another experienced instructor, Paul Hensley, operates **Wet Set** (❶ 998 871 0198 Ⓦ www.wetset.com) or you can **Dive in Puerto Morelos** (❶ 998 206 9084 Ⓦ www.diveinpuertomorelos.com). All three companies offer English-speaking instructors and guides.

Jardín Botánico Dr Alfredo Barrera Marín

The relaxing walking trails in this 50-hectare (124-acre) park will delight avid gardeners as well as those who just feel like a change from the beach. Precious hardwood trees, wild orchids, medicinal herbs, and cacti of all shapes and sizes abound. Visitors often spot wild deer, spider monkeys, parrots, toucans and other birds.

ⓐ Carretera 307 Km 33 ❶ 08.00–16.00 daily ❶ Birdwatchers admitted earlier on request; remember to check you have insect repellent with you and wear long trousers

Rancho Loma Bonita

This is one of the few places where you can arrange horse riding on the beach. Or you can choose to go quad-biking around a circuit that takes in the beach, jungle and mangroves. Tours can be booked direct, or from many hotels.

@ Carretera 307 Km 31 ☎ 998 887 5423

Tres Ríos Eco Park

Head south towards Playa del Carmen and at the halfway mark you will come across this nature park, so named because of the three rivers that run through it. Despite its billing, it really is more of an outdoor leisure park, with watersports, horse riding and football all on offer. There is also a fine stretch of long, white sandy beach here.

☎ 998 887 8077 🌐 www.tres-rios.com 🕒 09.00–17.00 daily

EXCURSIONS
Fishing

Just ask around the pier and you will find sport-fishing boats for hire for up to four people. A cheaper alternative is to negotiate with the locals and take one of the smaller, local fishing boats. High season is from March to August. Each May, an international tournament is held, with fishermen from around the world hunting the tuna, blue marlin and barracuda that can be found beyond the reef.

Sea Blue Snorkeling and Fishing runs deep-sea fishing tours and snorkel trips. ☎ 998 871 0611

Jungle tour

Kooltours takes small groups on one- and three-day tours where you can discover crystal-clear *cenotes* (natural wells), explore freshwater lagoons and hike to the cultural wonders left behind by the Maya – a world away from the bus-tour experience of Cancún.

@ Hotel Rancho Sak Ol ☎ 998 101 7696 🌐 www.kooltours.com

TAKING A BREAK

Le Café D'Amancia £ ❶ Great low-key, no-frills café where locals chat and often play chess over coffee and pastries. There is also an internet café upstairs. ⓐ Avenida Tulum, Lote 2 ❶ 998 206 9242 ⓛ 08.00–14.00 & 18.00–22.00 daily

David Lau's £ ❷ Fusion Mexican/Asian/Italian may seem unfathomable, but it works at this relaxed spot on the main square. Try the crab ragoon followed by Mandarin soup or the *Esmeralda* Pizza. ⓐ Avenida Tulum, on the *zócalo* (main square) ❶ 998 251 2531 ⓦ www.davidlaus.com ⓛ 11.00–23.00 daily

El Tío £ ❸ This cheap and cheerful diner is popular with locals and serves superb chicken soup and local specialities such as *sabutes*, *panuchos* and *tamales* (see page 98). ⓐ Avenida Rafael Melgar, opposite the lighthouse ⓛ 11.00–22.00 daily

Hola Asia ££ ❹ With a chef who grew up in Hong Kong, this little place offers a wonderful selection of Chinese, Japanese, Thai and Indian cuisine. Don't miss General Tso's Chicken – a local culinary legend. There's also a cosy rooftop bar with ocean views. ⓐ *Zócalo* ❶ 998 871 0679 ⓦ www.holaasia.com ⓛ 15.00–22.00 Mon & Wed–Sat, 13.00–22.00 Sun, closed Tues

John Gray's Kitchen ££ ❺ Near the Hotel Inglaterra is this relaxed gourmet restaurant with soft jazz and a varied menu that is always changing. Very popular. ⓐ Avenida Niños Héroes ❶ 998 871 0449 ⓛ 17.00–23.00 daily ❶ Reservations recommended

Los Pelicanos ££ ❻ With its ocean view and decent, authentic seafood menu, this is a friendly place for a dinner and is popular for cocktails. ⓐ Behind the *zócalo* ❶ 998 871 0014 ⓛ 10.00–23.00 daily

SHOPPING

The village has a general store, off-licence, chemist and ATM. In addition, **Alma Libre** on the *zócalo* is probably the best English-language bookshop in the whole of the Yucatán, offering everything from the classics to the latest blockbusters. It is also a great place for local maps. ⓐ *Zócalo* ⓣ 998 871 0713 ⓛ 10.00–15.00 & 18.00–21.00 Tues–Sun, closed Mon (Oct–June)

Try **Rosario & Marco's Art Shoppe** for arts, crafts and exhibitions featuring local artists. ⓐ Avenida Javier Rojo Gómez 14

Posada Amor ££ ❼ An all-round winner that serves breakfast, lunch and dinner in a relaxed family atmosphere. The Sunday brunch buffet is something of an institution. ⓐ Avenida Javier Rojo Gómez ⓣ 998 871 0033 ⓛ 07.00–22.00 daily

AFTER DARK

When it comes to all-night partying, visitors can go to Cancún or Playa del Carmen. But, before you head off, take a walk down to **La Caverna**, where local musicians gather to jam. Occasionally you may find a live band has blown in – just follow the noise. Come full moon, the locals may build a bonfire and throw a beach party.

⬤ *Puerto Morelos is a mecca for divers*

Playa del Carmen & Playacar

Much smaller than Cancún, Playa del Carmen, 64 km (40 miles) to the south, has a somewhat European atmosphere. Until the early 1980s, 'Playa' – as it is affectionately known – was just a fishing village, but today it is one of the fastest-growing communities in Mexico. A large international community holidays here, as well as a significant number of Mexicans and day trippers. In addition, enormous cruise ships dock here twice a week, swelling the local population.

Both Playa del Carmen and adjoining Playacar are centrally located on the Riviera Maya, roughly halfway between the big, bustling tourist resort of Cancún and Tulum's scenic, cliff-top Mayan fort. The ancient Maya appreciated the area's charms centuries before the Spaniards arrived in the 16th century and way before the tourists got here. Mayan ruins dot the coast, with a large concentration around Playa del Carmen.

In the centre of town is the pedestrianised **Avenida 5**, which runs through an area of boutique shops, good restaurants and interesting architecture. At its heart is the *zócalo*, or main square. West is **Avenida Juárez**, where the bus station, post office and a number of banks are located. North of Avenida 5 is where you will find most of the hotels, restaurants, bars and shops. The further you walk away from Avenida 5, the cheaper the restaurants and shops become and the quieter the beaches are. The Avenidas are numbered 5, 10, 15 and so on, so although, for example, 30 may sound far away from 5, it's only a short walk.

To the south of Playa del Carmen is the purpose-built, gated **Playacar** development, with its 18-hole golf course, large all-inclusive resorts, private rental apartments and residential area. Surrounded by some small Mayan archaeological sites, and with a few attractions of its own, it is still just a five-minute taxi ride from here to the centre of Playa del Carmen.

Playa del Carmen

BEACHES

Basking in the middle of the Riviera Maya, which stretches south of
Cancún all the way down to Tulum, Playa del Carmen and Playacar have
fine, white sand and crystal-clear water. The beaches shelve gradually
from the shore, making the sea seem like a large swimming pool.

Most of the resort's hotels are on or parallel to the coast, where the
white sand is beautifully clean. The pretty, long sweep of the main beach
of Playa del Carmen, with its bars and restaurants, narrows and then
gets progressively quieter to the north. Beyond the big yellow hotel of
Porto Real lies a wider stretch of sand where you can rent an umbrella
and a beach chair from one of the beach clubs. About a ten-minute walk

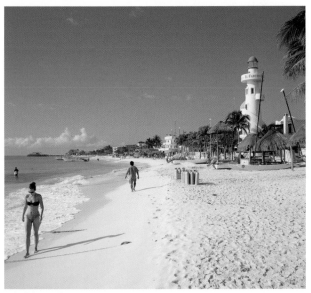

○ *The long sweep of beach at Playa del Carmen*

further north is **Coco Beach**, where there are several restaurants and a few dive shops. Nearby **Chunzubul Reef** provides both decent snorkelling and protection for local boats. Be aware, though, that much of the coral near to the shore here has been destroyed.

All Playa del Carmen's surrounding beaches are open to the public, with various access points along the shore. However, access becomes more difficult the further north you travel, where right of entry through private property is limited. The best way to explore is on foot along the sand, as most of the roads leading from the main highway to the shore between Puerto Morelos and Playa del Carmen are gated driveways.

After the main beach, the initial stretch to the north is named after resorts – Playa Tukan, Mamitas, Shangri-La, Zubul and Coco Beach. Bars and restaurants line this section of coast, so you need not walk far for refreshment. In addition, lifeguards are present, although safety precautions should always be followed.

Further north again are some of the most prized beaches on the Riviera Maya – the aptly named **Playa del Secreto** (Secret Beach) and **Playa Paraiso** (Paradise Beach), which are both 5 km (3 miles) wide. Sea turtles and crabs make regular visits to these big, white stretches of sand. They quickly merge into the beaches of **Punta Maroma** and **Punta Bete**, featuring both limestone and jungle, which seem designed for relaxing. Those with children might like to go to the part of the beach in front of the **Porto Real Resort**. A tiny section of coral here creates small pools of warm water, often populated with small fish that are both safe and interesting for small members of the family.

THINGS TO SEE & DO

Cenotes

There are many *cenotes* (natural freshwater wells connected to submerged caverns) where you can dive with excellent visibility. **Scuba Cenote** is run by Armando Elizalde, who operates guided adventures through the area's *cenotes*. ⓐ Calle 6 bis 235 ⓣ 984 131 2391 ⓦ www.scubacenote.com

Diving

Try diving in underwater caves, among dramatic stalactites, stalagmites and stunning coral formations with the British/Danish-run **Dive Mike** (ⓐ Calle 8, between Avenida 5 and Zona Federal Marítima ⓣ 984 803 1228 ⓦ www.divemike.com). There are also plenty of other dive shops to choose from in Playa del Carmen.

Golf

Playacar boasts the Yucatán coast's best golf course – the **Playacar Club de Golf**. This Robert von Hagge-designed, par 72 championship course has been sculpted out of the dense Mayan jungle, which makes for both scenic and challenging games. It can get terribly hot on Playacar's course, so you are advised to play either early or late in the day. Rates are reduced for twilight games (after 14.00).
ⓦ www.palace-resorts.com/playacar-golf-club

Jungle tour

Drive a quad bike through the jungle, swim in a clear, 18-m (60-ft) deep *cenote* and climb ancient Mayan ruins on a two-hour tour.
ATV Explorer ⓐ Carretera 307 ⓣ 984 873 1626
ⓦ www.atvexplorer.com

Xaman-Ha Aviary

Visitors can walk along trails surrounded by colourful birds, including parrots and toucans, flamingos and scarlet macaws as well as other wildlife such as iguanas and butterflies.
ⓐ Paseo Xaman-Ha, Playacar ⓣ 984 873 0330
ⓦ www.aviarioxamanha.com/english ⓛ 09.00–17.00 daily

EXCURSIONS
Cozumel

Take a boat trip to the beautiful island of Cozumel (see page 58), little over half an hour away. Easily visited on a day trip, it is a haven for divers and nature lovers.

Fishing

Although fishing trips on small *pangas* (an open fishing boat) – either
full or half day – are available from the beach in Playa del Carmen, a
much wider choice, on bigger boats, is on offer from Puerto Aventuras'
marina, just 20 minutes south. These usually include (it's worth checking) a captain and mate, bait, tackle, fish filleting and light refreshments.

This part of the coast is particularly good for deep-sea fishing
because the nearby island of Cozumel forces big fish to run close to
the shore. Potential impressive catches include sailfish (high season

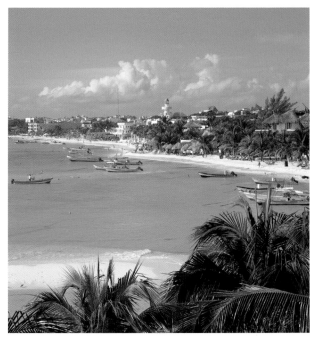

🔺 *Playa del Carmen – from fishing village to lively Caribbean sunscape*

March–July, but available year-round) and billfish (March–September). Blue and white marlin are common, and tuna and reef fish can be caught all year.

Swimming with dolphins

Swim and play with bottlenose dolphins at Parque Nizuc and learn about their behaviour from knowledgeable trainers. Participants must be at least 1.2 m (4 ft) tall and children must be accompanied by an adult (maximum of two children per adult).

ⓐ Parque Nizuc, Cancún (see page 19)

TAKING A BREAK

Java Joe's £ ❶ A local institution. Excellent coffees, from espressos to iced mochas, as well as pastries, sandwiches and bagels.
ⓐ Calle 10, between Avenidas 5 and 10 ❶ 984 876 2694
Ⓦ www.javajoes.net ❶ 06.30–23.00 daily

Sabor! £ ❷ Pastries, coffees and vegetarian health foods are prepared and served by the owners. ⓐ Avenida 5, between Calles 2 and 4
❶ 18.00–23.00 daily

Los Almendros ££ ❸ This small, rustic, family-owned restaurant offers traditional Yucatán food at very affordable prices. ⓐ Avenida 10 and Calle 6 ❶ 08.00–24.00 daily

Da Gabi Ristorante ££ ❹ Choose from Italian dishes such as oven-baked pizza and home-made fettuccini or go for fresh seafood or a T-bone steak. ⓐ Avenida 5 and Calle 12 ❶ 984 873 0048
❶ 12.00–24.00 daily

The Lazy Lizard ££ ❺ A friendly café where you can enjoy international and Mexican food in a pretty spot with almond trees.
ⓐ Avenida 5, between Calles 2 and 4 ❶ 07.00–23.00 daily

AFTER DARK

Limones ££ ❻ French fusion cuisine is served in a romantic setting with candlelit tables and fountains. The daily specials are usually hard to fault. ⓐ Avenida 5 and Calle 6 ⓣ 984 873 0526 ⓛ 17.00–22.30 daily

Sur ££ ❼ A fashionable Argentinian restaurant with a colonial feel owing to the hardwood floors, swirling fans and leafy foliage. Traditional Latin staples, pizza and plenty of meat dishes, all reasonably priced. ⓐ Avenida 5, between Calles 12 and 14 ⓛ 11.00–24.00 daily

Byblos £££ ❽ Elegant French restaurant complete with linen tablecloths. Escargots, French onion soup and lobster medallions in cream sauce are all on the menu and there is a good wine list. ⓐ Calle 14, between Avenidas 5 and 10 ⓣ 984 803 1790 ⓛ 18.00–01.00 Mon–Sat, closed Sun

Casa Mediterránea £££ ❾ Wonderful home-made Italian dishes are prepared using the freshest ingredients. Everything is made to order and served by the friendly staff. ⓐ Avenida 5, between Calles 6 and 8 ⓣ 984 876 3926 ⓛ 13.30–23.00 Wed–Mon, closed Tues

Media Luna £££ ❿ One of Playa's most popular restaurants offers beautifully prepared seafood, pasta and vegetarian dishes in an attractive setting. ⓐ Avenida 5, between Calles 12 and 14 ⓣ 984 873 0526 ⓛ 08.00–23.00 daily

Yaxche Maya Cuisine £££ ⓫ An award-winning restaurant that works with the local Mayan community. It offers a unique menu that is a fusion of Mayan, Yucatán and European cuisine, and also holds special events and theme-dinner nights. ⓐ Calle 8, between Avenidas 5 and 10 ⓣ 984 873 2502 ⓛ 12.00–24.00 daily

Many of the restaurants in Playa del Carmen double as bars and night-clubs later in the evening. The Avenida 5 'strip' is full of bars and clubs.

Deseo Lounge 🔟 has a rooftop bar with a small pool, a DJ playing ambient music – and beds. The drinks aren't cheap, but at least they are brought to you while you remain horizontal (🅐 Avenida 5 and Calle 12). **Alux** 🔟 (pronounced 'Ah-loosh') is a unique bar, restaurant and club inside a cave, complete with water, stalagmites, live music and shows (🅐 Avenida Juárez, three blocks west of Carretera 307 🕒 Tues–Sun, closed Mon). Chill out in the Moroccan lounge or on the bamboo beach beds of the **Blue Parrot** 🔟 while you enjoy live music, fire dancers and DJs (🅐 Calle 12 🆆 www.blueparrot.com). **Tequila Barrel** 🔟 is friendly, and a great place for people-watching, with more than 100 different tequilas to choose from (🅐 Avenida 5, between Calles 10 and 12). The rooftop bar at **Hotel Básico** 🔟 is another hangout for resident funksters with cocktails, cabanas and hammocks adding to a chilled-out vibe, while local DJs spin an eclectic soundtrack (🅐 Calle 10, between Avenida 5 and 10 Norte 🆆 www.hotelbasico.com).

SHOPPING

Most of Playa del Carmen's shops are on the bustling pedestrianised main strip that runs parallel to the beach: Avenida 5 (also known as 'Quinta Avenida'). Popular items are jewellery, hammocks, panama hats and embroidered clothing.

The **Etoncha Amber Gallery** sells gemstones from Chiapas, notably prized amber (🅐 Avenida 5, between Calles 8 and 10). **Blue Planet** is a fashion time warp with 1970s-style beachwear (🅐 Avenida 5, between Calles 10 and 12). **La Calaca** has a good collection of wooden masks and carvings (🅐 Avenida 5 and Calle 5) and **Amber Mexicano** sells amber jewellery that is made by a local designer (🅐 Avenida 5, between Calles 4 and 6). For more sophisticated, upmarket clothing, try **Crunch** (🅐 Avenida 5, between Calles 6 and 8).

In Playacar, the two main centres for shopping are **Paseo del Carmen** and **Plaza Playacar**.

Puerto Aventuras

Just 15 minutes from Playa del Carmen, and conveniently located for exploring the Riviera Maya, Puerto Aventuras is a gated development that is a world away from the bigger resorts on the coast. This 365-hectare (900-acre) private facility has been constructed around a large marina, complete with beach club, international restaurants, dive centre and nine-hole golf course.

Known simply as 'Puerto' by locals, the contained community prides itself on its 24-hour security. It is safe to walk or drive around at night, street sellers are controlled, and you will find none of the rowdy behaviour often on display in the nearby resorts of Playa del Carmen and Cancún. With just a handful of larger hotels, much of the accommodation is to be found in apartments and villas, all of which makes Puerto Aventuras popular with families.

BEACHES

The development of Puerto Aventuras is made up of two sheltered coves with powdery white sand. **Fátima Bay** at the centre of the resort covers more than 2.5 km (1¹/₂ miles) of shore from **Chac Hal Al** to the Grand Peninsula. This wide expanse of beach, with calm waters and a nearby reef, boasts various watersports and other activities. Here, the Omni Hotel serves as a beach club, open to anyone who buys a drink.

To the north is the smaller **Chan Yu Yum** with the all-inclusive Sunscape Puerto Aventuras hotel (formerly the Oasis); access to the beach is restricted to guests staying in the immediate area. Chac Hal Al to the south is an inlet that forms a nature reserve with mostly exclusive accommodation.

Further afield, halfway to Xcaret, is **Paamul**. This peaceful beach is perfect for relaxation and those who want to dive or participate in watersports. Nature lovers will appreciate the sea turtles that come here to lay their eggs between May and July.

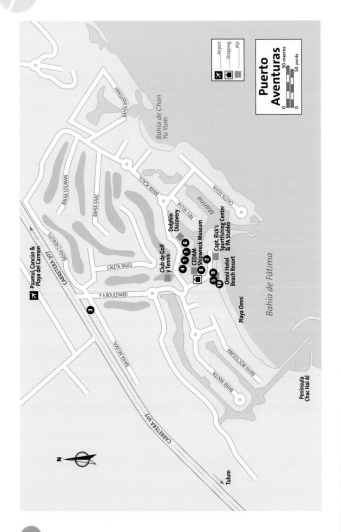

Puerto Aventuras

THINGS TO SEE & DO

CEDAM Shipwreck Museum

Navigating this stretch of coast has always been notoriously dangerous due to the Great Maya Reef offshore. This museum shows treasures found on 18th-century shipwrecks.

🅐 Behind the marina 🕿 984 873 5000 🕘 10.00–13.00 daily
ℹ Donations welcome

Golf

The 18-hole course here is set in lush jungle that provides a cool relief from the heat of the day. Rental clubs and carts are available and there is a putting green.

Club de Golf y Tennis 🅐 Behind the marina 🕿 984 873 5109
ℹ Green fees approximately US$88; weekly rates available. No reservations required; credit cards not accepted

Marina

The marina here is the biggest on the Riviera Maya and it is the only deep-water facility on the mainland between Cancún and Belize City. Stroll around the pretty oceanfront location, stop for a coffee or something stronger, or even charter a boat. Choose a leisurely sail on a catamaran, or go snorkelling in the clear waters of the beaches and coves nearby. Most tours include lunch and time for relaxing.

🕿 984 873 5108 🌐 www.travelpuertoaventuras.com/marina.htm

Scuba diving

Ocean diving, *cenote* diving and instruction are available with **Dive Aventuras** located inside the Omni Beach Resort in the marina. The reef is little more than 90 m (100 yds) from the beach. The first wall, only 20 m (66 ft) deep, offers a variety of underwater sites with plenty to see. The more adventurous can tackle a second wall that drops 40 m (130 ft) and even further.

🕿 984 873 5031 🌐 www.diveaventuras.com

Tennis

Active types can play on synthetic grass courts surrounded by attractive vegetation at the resort's golf and tennis club. Discounted weekly and monthly rates are available and lessons can be arranged.

Club de Golf y Tennis ⓐ Behind the marina ❶ 984 873 5109 ⏱ 08.30–dusk daily

EXCURSIONS

Cancún

This mega-resort is less than an hour away. Make a trip for a larger-than-life experience, but don't expect much relaxation (see page 15).

Cozumel

This nearby island is easily accessible, with daily departures from the marina. Cozumel's beaches and rich underwater life are the main attractions, particularly the diving and snorkelling (see page 58).

Fishing

Puerto Aventuras is a world-class centre for sport fishing, home to enticing catches of sailfish, marlin, dorado (mahi-mahi), barracuda and tuna. Success is virtually guaranteed, thanks partly to the proximity of the grounds to Puerto Aventuras itself. Those who opt for the more leisurely pursuit of bottom fishing can look forward to reeling in snapper. Most fishing trips will accommodate non-fishers, who can snorkel and swim from the boat. At the end of your fishing trip, ask the crew to fillet your catch – you can take it home for supper. Both full- and half-day trips are available from **Capt. Rick's Sportfishing Center**.
ⓐ Marina, past the Omni Hotel on your right ❶ 984 873 5195 ⓦ www.fishyucatan.com ⏱ 08.00–17.00 daily ❗ Credit cards accepted

Horse riding

Take a gentle, scenic ride through the jungle, then swim or snorkel (equipment provided) in the cooling waters of *cenotes* (natural wells), enjoy a picnic lunch and spot butterflies and iguanas. The whole trip

⬤ *One of the many* cenotes *in the Yucatán*

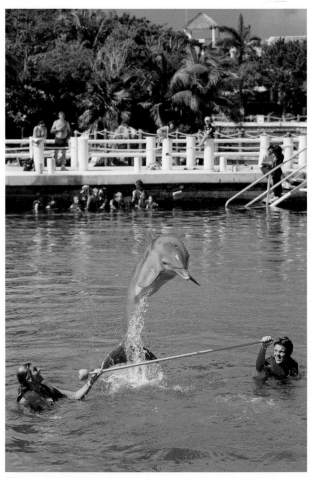

⬥ *Dolphins abound at Dolphin Discovery*

takes four hours door to door, available through **P A Stables**.
🅐 On the right past the Omni Hotel, office is in Capt. Rick's Sportfishing Center 🕾 984 873 5035 ❶ Credit cards not accepted

Playa del Carmen
Just 15 minutes to the north, this lively resort is worth a visit for its selection of restaurants and shops, or for change of scene (see page 40).

Swimming with dolphins
Dolphins as well as two manatees – Romeo and Juliet – can be seen in captivity at **Dolphin Discovery**.
🅐 Marina 🕾 998 849 4748 🌐 www.dolphindiscovery.com
🕒 09.00–18.00 daily ❶ Advance booking recommended; credit cards accepted

Tulum
These spectacular, cliff-top ruins are just 25 minutes to the south of the resort (see page 78).

TAKING A BREAK

Caribana £ ❶ This simple place serves Mayan-inspired cuisine, including a great-value set meal of soup, main course with salad and a soft drink.
🅐 Behind the Italian Bakery, Plaza Marina Edificio A 8A and B 🕾 984 873 5175 🕒 08.00–20.00 Mon–Sat, closed Sun ❶ Credit cards not accepted

Italian Bakery £ ❷ This is *the* place for breakfast and it's not a bad spot for lunch and dinner either. 🅐 Off the Puerto Aventuras plaza 🕒 Daily ❶ Credit cards not accepted

Taco Paco £ ❸ Don't miss the Mexican food dished up at this much-loved roadside food stand. Owner Paco's seafood tacos are legendary. 🅐 Pemex station at entrance to Puerto Aventuras and Carretera 307 🕒 From 11.00, most days ❶ Credit cards not accepted

Arigato ££ ❹ Only fresh fish bought that day from local fishermen will do for the owner of this excellent, beachfront sushi restaurant. Curries, salads and sandwiches are also on offer. ⓐ Behind the marina, Plaza Marina Edificio C 3 ❶ 984 801 0196 ❶ 13.30–22.00 daily ❶ Credit cards not accepted

Café Ole ££ ❺ This popular and friendly terrace café has a menu featuring everything from chicken *chimichurri* to high-quality steaks, with daily specials. On Sundays in high season, there is live music. ⓐ Opposite the Omni Hotel ❶ 984 873 5125 ❶ 08.00–23.00 daily

AFTER DARK

No one really goes to Puerto Aventuras for the nightlife; if you are looking for late nights or discos, nearby Playa del Carmen is probably your best bet. That said, there are a handful of bars where you can enjoy a cocktail or a beer, some of which offer entertainment.

A good place to start is one of the thatched beachside *palapas* near the marina. The **Pina Colada Jacuzzi Beach Bar**, part of the Omni Hotel, is in a scenic spot overlooking the Caribbean Sea and a great place for a tropical cocktail, but it does close at 19.00.

The Pub £ ❻ An expat aura prevails here, with a large selection of beers and well-priced food, ranging from pizza and burgers to delicious barbecue ribs. ⓐ Set back from the marina ❶ 984 873 5130 ❶ 08.00–24.00 daily

Golden Dragon ££ ❼ The Caribana restaurant (see page 55) transforms nightly into an Asian eatery serving mostly Chinese cuisine. Take out or eat in. ⓐ Behind the Italian Bakery, Plaza Marina Edificio A 8A and B ❶ 984 873 5175

Richard's Quarter Deck ££ ❽ A basic diet of steak, seafood and pizza, along with a salad bar, is served up here, but specials and occasional barbecues may be worth a look. The owner is a bit of a 'character' but he serves a good steak – the barbecued prawns are good too.
ⓐ Plaza Marina Edificio E 3B, on the marina ❶ 984 873 5086
🕒 Lunch and dinner

Xenote ££ ❾ If you are craving air conditioning and wish to try decent Mayan specialities, Xenote is a solid choice. There is also a lively *palapa* bar, open for breakfast, lunch and dinner. ⓐ Inside the Omni Hotel
❶ 984 875 1950 🕒 From 08.00 daily

Da Vinci £££ ❿ Fine renditions of Italian specialities are served in a breezy, oceanfront setting at the Omni Hotel. The fish dishes are always über-fresh. Request *al dente* to avoid overcooked pasta. ⓐ Omni Hotel, Puerto Juárez Km 269.5 ❶ 984 875 1950 🕒 18.00–23.00 daily

SHOPPING

Those who are self-catering can stock up in one of the food shops in Puerto Aventuras, although Playa del Carmen has a lot more choice. Several boutiques and gift shops can be found around the marina. **Arte Maya** sells clothes and accessories created by a Mexican designer. **P A Boutique and Gift Shop** is more of a one-stop shop, selling everything from beachwear to postcards and film to snorkelling gear.

Cozumel

Just 19 km (12 miles) from the coast, the island of Cozumel is fringed by pretty beaches and spectacular coral reefs that are home to thousands of tropical fish. Oceanographer Jacques Cousteau introduced Cozumel to the world in 1961 and it has been one of the top global diving destinations ever since. Understandably, many of the activities on the island are water-based, whether it is swimming in the clear blue waters, snorkelling over the reefs or taking a scenic boat ride. There is also wonderful wildlife to be seen, and inland areas of jungle and mangroves.

Ferries from the mainland and large cruise ships dock in **San Miguel**, the only built-up area on Cozumel. This small town is also home to almost all of the island's bars, shops and restaurants.

BEACHES

One continuous white sand beach stretches all around the island. The best snorkelling is on the western side, where equipment and facilities are offered by the many beach clubs, and if you buy a drink or two you can use the sunloungers and umbrellas. The beaches on the east face the open sea and are often deserted, although you will need transportation to get to them. One of the most beautiful beaches is **Playa San Francisco**. On the main part of the beach there are restaurants and watersports, but there is a quieter stretch a few kilometres south at **Playa Palancar**. North of San Miguel, **Playa San Juan** is the best place for swimmers and those keen on watersports.

THINGS TO SEE & DO

ATV tours

Explore caves, forests, beaches and a Mayan ruin as you venture off-road on a two-hour ATV tour with **Wild Tours**.

ⓘ 987 872 5876/188 497 4283 Ⓦ www.wild-tours.com

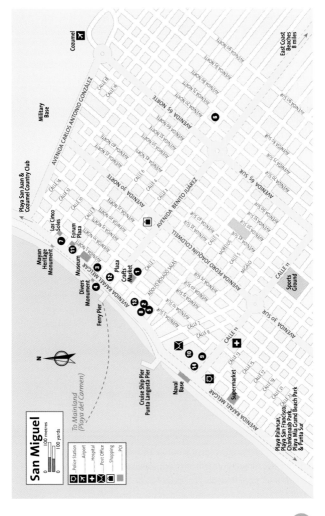

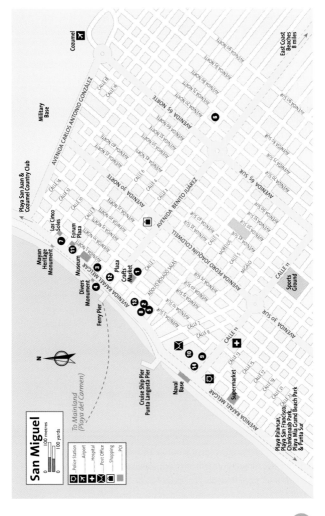

Boat trips

Drop 30 m (100 ft) beneath the waves and explore the reefs in the **Atlantis Submarine** (W www.atlantisadventures.com). Take a three-hour trip on a glass-bottomed boat to snorkelling spots or enjoy a sunset cruise, with music and cocktails.

Chankanaab Park

Go diving and snorkelling and even swim with dolphins at this marine park and aquarium that features turtles, coral and fish.
ⓐ Carretera Costera Sur Km 9.5 W www.cozumelparks.com.mx

Diving

The island has world-class diving of all descriptions, whether you want lessons or specialised cavern trips. **Cozumel-Diving Net** is a website listing dive companies on the island (W http://cozumel-diving.net).

Fishing

The island is a dream for those who love to fish. Go fly fishing for snapper, bonefish and barracuda or take a deep-sea fishing trip and try your luck with marlin, dorado or tuna. The best fishing months are February to July.

Golf

The par 72 golf course at the **Cozumel Country Club** provides challenges for players of all handicaps, and is surrounded by mangroves and tropical rainforest.
ⓣ 987 872 9570 W www.cozumelcountryclub.com.mx

Punta Sur

A park and nature reserve set in a lagoon and marine environment, with mangrove jungles, coastal dunes and white sand beaches where you can see all types of flora and fauna, including crocodiles, iguanas, orchids and more than 200 species of birds.
ⓣ 987 872 0914 W www.cozumelparks.com.mx

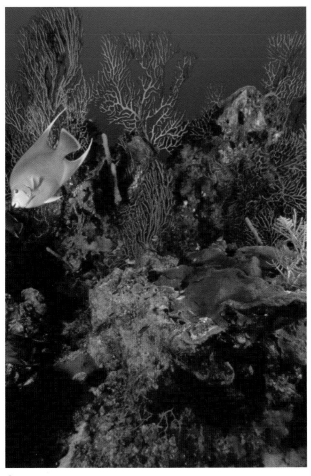

◆ *A coral reef off Cozumel*

Snuba

If you love to snorkel, but are unsure about diving, why not try 'snuba', a combination of the two? Allowing you to breathe underwater, it is suitable for children over eight.

Snuba Cozumel ☎ 987 878 4647 🌐 www.snubacozumel.net

Watersports

A range of watersports is on offer at **Playa Mía Grand Beach Park**, from snorkel tours to parasailing. Children love the banana rides, water trampoline and 'beach iceberg'.

📧 info@playamia.com

EXCURSIONS

Playa del Carmen (see page 40) on the mainland can be reached in just 35 minutes on one of the fast boats. Or why not take a day trip to see the spectacular sacred site of Tulum (see page 78)?

TAKING A BREAK

Casa Denis £ ❶ A great-value local spot that has been serving Yucatán specialities since the 1940s. Grab an outside table and a monumental torta. 🏠 Calle 1 Sur 132, between Avenidas 5 and 10 ☎ 987 872 0067 🌐 www.casadenis.com 🕙 11.30–22.00 daily

Cocos Cozumel £ ❷ Fantastic American-style breakfasts that will set you up for a day of activities. Eggs, muffins, pancakes and waffles are decadent and delicious. 🏠 Avenida 5 Sur 180 ☎ 987 872 0241 🕙 06.00–12.00 Tues–Sun, closed Mon

Zermaatt £ ❸ A bakery with delicious goodies, as well as fresh breads. 🏠 Avenida 5, between Calles 2 and 4 🕙 07.00–20.00 daily

Prima £££ ❹ Not surprisingly, it is the fresh fish and seafood conjured with Italian flair at this local trattoria. The pesto and Alfredo sauces are

rich and creamy, while the salads are bountiful and healthy.
Save room for the key lime pie. ⓐ El Cantil, Avenida Rafael Melgar
ⓣ 987 872 4242 ⓦ www.primacozumel.com ⓛ 17.00–22.30 daily

AFTER DARK

French Quarter £–££ ❺ Big portions of Cajun food are served inside or
on the roof terrace. Try 'gumbo' or the house special of filet mignon with
red-onion marmalade. ⓐ Avenida 5, between Calle Adolfo Rosado Salas
and Calle 3 ⓣ 987 872 6321 ⓛ 17.00–24.00 Wed–Mon, closed Tues

El Moro ££ ❻ People come to this great backstreet restaurant for the
food and not the décor, which is very basic. Excellent Mexican dishes and
seafood. The lime soup and lobster are particularly good. ⓐ Avenida 75
Norte, between Calles 2 and 4 ⓣ 987 872 3029 ⓛ 13.00–23.00 Fri–Wed,
closed Thur

Pancho's Backyard ££ ❼ The beautiful courtyard makes this a romantic
spot to eat. Mexican dishes, steak and seafood are served by friendly
staff. ⓐ Los Cincos Soles Mall, Avenida Rafael Melgar 27 ⓣ 987 872 2141
ⓛ 10.00–23.00 Mon–Fri, 18.00–23.00 Sat & Sun

Pepe's Grill ££–£££ ❽ Large, popular place overlooking the bay, with live
guitar music. Excellent grilled steaks and seafood and a children's menu.
ⓐ Avenida Rafael Melgar and Adolfo Rosado Salas ⓣ 987 872 0213
ⓘ Reservations recommended ⓛ 17.00–23.30 daily

Evening entertainment begins and ends early here. Yet the nightclubs
are pretty lively and friendly, many featuring live music. Most venues are
just north of the main plaza on Avenida Rafael Melgar or in the Punta
Langosta shopping centre. Some larger resorts have their own discos.
Tequila Lounge ❾ is a chic bar with a fantastic location on the seafront.
Watch the sunset while sipping a cocktail and listening to lounge music
(ⓐ Avenida Rafael Melgar and Calle 11 ⓣ 987 872 4421). **Carlos and**

Charlie's ❿ is a lively, mainstream spot open until the early hours on the waterfront (🅰 Punta Langosta Mall).

There is an array of American-style drinking dens along Avenida Rafael Melgar, including **Carlos 'n' Charlies**, **Señor Frogs** and the ubiquitous **Hard Rock Café**.

At **Havana Club** ⓫ go for live jazz, cocktails and Cuban or Mexican cigars, but try to avoid the imported spirits, which are expensive (🅰 Avenida Rafael Melgar 37B, between Calles 6 and 8 ☎ 987 872 1268). Visit **Joe's Reggae Bar** ⓬ for reggae dancing and salsa until dawn (🅰 Avenida Rafael Melgar, at the ferry pier ☎ 987 872 3275).

La Pura Vida ⓭ is a Latin club that plays salsa, samba and merengue until the early hours (🅰 Avenida 5 and Adolfo Rosado Salas ☎ 987 878 7831), while the **Neptuno Dance Club** ⓮ is Cozumel's best-known and oldest disco, with a light-and-laser show to entertain (🅰 Avenida Rafael Melgar and Calle 11 ☎ 987 872 1537).

SHOPPING

Thanks to the large cruise ships that visit Cozumel, there are lots of shops – chiefly selling clothes and jewellery. The main shopping areas are along the waterfront and from the ferry pier back towards the main town square, which is known variously as Plaza del Sol, Plaza San Miguel or just the Plaza! Behind this square there is a **Crafts Market** selling all kinds of souvenirs.

Many shops, particularly those near the cruise-ship passenger terminal at **Punta Langosta Pier**, offer duty-free goods. They claim that customers can make large savings, but the items are often quite expensive, so be sure to compare prices.

There is a wide selection of crafts, as well as local jewellery and embroidered clothing, at **Los Cinco Soles** (🅰 Avenida Rafael Melgar Norte 27 ☎ 987 872 0132). **Forum Plaza** has a range of shops selling clothes and designer goods, as well as an interactive jewellery workshop.

Akumal

This small resort, whose name means 'place of the turtle' in Mayan, lies in the heart of the Riviera Maya. Once a huge coconut plantation, Akumal became a tourist centre way back in the 1950s when it was established as an exclusive centre for divers. The Mayan population was moved to a new town on the other side of the motorway, and today the community is one of the most Americanised on this stretch of coast.

Despite being the Riviera Maya's oldest resort, Akumal is still something of a secret and maintains a relaxed atmosphere. Its main attractions are the lovely beaches, spectacular lagoon and lush jungle. Abundant bird and animal life surrounds the resort, and can be spotted either on short walks and bike trips or on longer, organised tours.

BEACHES

The beaches around Akumal all have fine, white sand and a coral reef close to the shore, which makes for calm waters as well as great snorkelling. The focus of the resort is **Akumal Bay**, where there are good watersports and facilities. This beach can get very crowded during holidays and weekends. To the north, the quieter **Half Moon Bay** has a pretty, crescent-shaped beach with some rocks.

Even quieter is **Jade Beach**, 2.5 km (1½ miles) south of Akumal Bay and reached by an attractive, easy 20-minute walk along the coast. The next beach south is **South Akumal**, a gated community of mostly beachfront villas. Finally, **Aventuras Akumal**, a lovely long stretch of beach, is 6.5 km (4 miles) south of Akumal itself. The northern part of this beach has a hotel whose amenities are available for a fee.

THINGS TO SEE & DO

Akumal Kid's Club
Children up to ten years old can participate in either morning or evening activities, such as painting, beach games and nature trips.

ⓐ Akumal Bay, near Lol-Ha Snack Bar ⓔ info@akumaldirect.com
🕐 09.00–14.00 & 18.00–21.00 daily ❶ Hourly rates per child; prepaid day rates are cheaper

Bike rides

Akumal is small enough to be explored by bicycle. Make a tour around the town, visiting beaches and the lagoon, or take a longer trip to the jungle. Bike hire available from **Travel Services Akumal**.
ⓐ Akumal Bay, by Akumal Dive Shop ❶ 984 875 9030/31

Diving

Clear waters and uncrowded conditions make Akumal a great dive experience, especially for beginners. Contact the **Akumal Dive Centre** for more information on its range of tours.
❶ 984 875 9032 ⓦ www.akumaldiveshop.com

Fishing

Sport fishing is big in Akumal, where all fish are 'catch and release'. King fish, tuna, sailfish and marlin are popular hauls in the main season between April and July. Two-hour trips throughout the year are also possible with **Akumal Dive Adventure**.
❶ 984 875 9157 🕐 08.00–17.00 daily ❶ Reservations advised

Turtle Walk

Enjoy the rare experience of seeing turtles land on the beach to dig their nest and lay eggs. You can also help biologists record important information and to protect these fascinating creatures. Turtle sightings are not guaranteed, and, even if you do encounter one, it may take two hours before she returns to the sea, so it is necessary to be patient. Wear insect repellent and shoes suitable for the beach. Bring drinking water, and, for evening tours, a torch. Make sure your hands are clean, as you may be asked to help one of the creatures. You may also be interested in doing a good deed and adopting a turtle for a small sum from the **Centro Ecológico de Akumal** (CEA).

◆ *Swimming with turtles at Centro Ecológico de Akumal*

ⓐ Centro Ecológico de Akumal ☏ 984 875 9095 🌐 www.ceakumal.org
🕐 14.00–18.00 Mon, 08.00–14.00 & 16.00–18.00 Tues–Fri, 10.00–14.00
Sat; walks Mon–Sat at 20.00 (May–Sept), closed Sun ❶ Reservations
recommended

Yal Kú Lagoon

The clear waters of this narrow lagoon, sandwiched between
dense mangroves and the sea, invite swimming and snorkelling.
Birds such as pelicans and herons can be spotted on its tiny islands,
while towards the mouth you may see stingrays and feeding sea
turtles. This special place is also very fragile and is threatened by
tourist traffic.

ⓐ North Akumal, 2 km (1¼ miles) from Akumal Bay 🕐 08.00–17.00 daily
❶ Do not use sunscreen as it pollutes the aquatic life – if you burn easily,
wear a T-shirt; entrance fee payable

EXCURSIONS

Cancún

A little over 95 km (60 miles) away, this huge holiday resort with lots of
entertainment is easily reached on a day trip (see page 15).

Cozumel

The ferry to the lovely island of Cozumel, known for its beaches and
sealife (see page 58), leaves 32 km (20 miles) north of Playa del Carmen.
A visit is easily possible as a day trip.

Puerto Aventuras

Just 16 km (10 miles) away, Puerto Aventuras offers activities such as golf
and tennis as well as a marina (see page 49).

Robinson Crusoe tours

There are several 'Robinson Crusoe' tours, all of which last most of the
day, taking in a secluded bay for swimming, snorkelling and fishing and
including a fresh fish lunch.

ⓐ Akumal Dive Shop ☎ 984 875 9032 ⓦ www.akumaldiveshop.com
ⓘ Reservations recommended

Tulum
The ancient Mayan site (see page 78) has a stunning Caribbean setting and is less than an hour away by car.

> **SHOPPING**
>
> For souvenirs, try any of the small **open-air markets** along the main coast road, both north and south of Akumal. Look for hammocks, pottery and local crafts, and expect to bargain. Self-caterers may be interested in the **Farmer's Market**, which is open Wednesdays and Saturdays at the entrance to Akumal. It offers a wonderful variety of tropical fruits and fresh vegetables.
>
> The **Mexico Maya Gift Shop** in Akumal Bay has a good range of gifts, including jewellery. Souvenirs and beachwear can be found at the **Oshun Gift Shop** (ⓐ On the left, just outside Akumal's main entrance).

TAKING A BREAK

Lucy's Kitchen £ Fish tacos and heavenly ice cream, home-made on the premises, are the major draw at this cheerful café. ⓐ Plaza Ukana I ⓦ www.lucyskitchen.net 🕒 11.00–17.30 Mon–Sat, closed Sun

Turtle Bay Bakery £ A delightful spot and the local favourite for breakfast such as home-made muffins, fresh fruit or eggs cooked whichever way you like them. ⓐ Akumal Bay 🕒 07.00–15.00 daily (& 18.00–21.00 Tues–Sat)

La Buena Vida ££ The kitchen specialises in Caribbean, Mayan and seafood dishes. Lunch is served under thatched umbrellas on the beach. Outside are two crow's nests, which offer great views of the coast.

The bar, with its sand floors and swings, is particularly popular late at night. ⓐ Half Moon Bay ⓣ 984 875 6061

La Cueva del Pescador ££ 'The Cave of Fish', which specialises in local cuisine, is deservedly popular. It is a great place for a cold beer or glass of wine and freshly grilled fish or seafood tacos. The food is good as well as being reasonably priced. ⓐ Next to Turtle Bay ⓛ 12.00–16.00 & 18.00–24.00 daily

Que Onda Restaurant ££ An intimate establishment in a lovely tropical jungle location near the Yal Kú Lagoon. Italian dishes and seafood are the specialities. ⓦ www.queondaakumel.com ⓛ 14.00–22.30 Wed–Mon, closed Tues

Lol Ha Restaurant £££ The longest running of all Akumal restaurants is still the most successful. The menu features seafood, steak and Mexican dishes, and there is an adjoining pizza restaurant and beach bar serving snacks. Go for a Happy Hour at 17.30–18.30. ⓐ Akumal Bay ⓛ 07.30–22.00 daily ⓘ Entertainment several nights a week, such as live jazz or folk dancing

ⓞ *Taxis waiting for fares in Mexico City*

EXCURSIONS
Out & about

Pre-Hispanic culture

Way before the Spanish arrived, advanced cultures such as the Aztecs and Maya left their mark all over Mexico. Although it's impossible to see everything in one visit, the Yucatán makes a great base for exploring the country's rich history of ancient civilisations, particularly as there are some spectacular archaeological sites within easy reach of the main resorts along the Caribbean coast.

CHICHÉN ITZÁ

This site was an important commercial and ceremonial centre, believed to have been constructed between AD 600 and the end of the first millennium. The Maya were advanced mathematicians, engineers and astronomers, and this is evident in the buildings that remain here. For the best experience, try to arrive as early as possible, as the site gets extremely crowded from 11.00 onwards. Bear in mind that the heat of the sun can be unbearable in the middle of the day and there is little shade.

You can still explore the magnificent pyramid-shaped temple known as **El Castillo**, which was dedicated to the feathered serpent god Kukulkán. Some think that the snake that can be seen moving over the pyramid on both equinoxes (21 September and 21 March) was designed as a signal to begin the planting and subsequent harvest of crops.

Also not to be missed are the remains of the recreational **Jego de Pelota** ('Ball Court'), which was larger than a modern football pitch, with goals that were raised 6 m (20 ft) up in the air! It is believed that war captives were sometimes forced to play, and, although nobody knows if it was the winners or losers who were then sacrificed, we do know that their heads, along with countless others, were displayed on spikes on the **Tzompantli** ('Wall of Skulls').

However, not all sacrificial victims ended up there. The **Cenote Sagrado** ('Sacred Well') is an impressive natural well, 90 m (98 yds) in diameter, within which explorers have found not just pieces of gold and jade jewellery, but even the skeletons of children. As you peer over the

⬥ *Pyramid of Kukulcán in Chichén Itzá*

edge into the 20-m (66-ft) deep abyss, you can only imagine the horror the condemned faced before they were sacrificed to the rain gods.

ⓐ 170 km (105½ miles; around three hours) from Cancún, on the road to Mérida **ⓛ** 08.00–17.00 daily **ⓘ** Buses depart frequently from Cancún and the main resorts along the Riviera Maya, mostly as part of organised tours; from Cozumel and Isla Mujeres, many tourists opt for a same-day flight package, which is almost as cheap and much less tiring

COBÁ

This hugely important Mayan site, dating from AD 600 to 900, covers more than 80 sq km (31 sq miles), and it is estimated that between 50,000 and 100,000 people lived here. The Mayan ruins at Cobá are unique in that they have not really been restored in any way – the jungle

ⵔ *Sunset at Chichén Itzá*

has just been cleared from around them. Only a few of the estimated 6,500 structures have been uncovered, but those that have been revealed are impressive and astonishingly beautiful. Experts believe that Cobá was probably an important trading post between the Caribbean coast and the inland cities.

It is a steep climb to the top of the **Nohoch Mul pyramid** (the tallest in the Yucatán at over 42 m/138 ft), but the view from the top is well worth it. Kilometre after kilometre of jungle canopy is broken up only by **Lake Macanox** and the tops of temples and other pyramids jutting above the treetops – testament to the number of structural wonders still to be revealed. At the top of Nohoch Mul is a small temple with two little carvings that are echoed in the ruins at Tulum (see page 78), though no one is quite sure what their meaning is.

One of the most intriguing features of Cobá is the raised network of wide roads known as *sacbes* (white roads), which long ago stretched across the entire Yucatán Peninsula. Like Roman roads, these were built in straight lines from A to B, and they were constructed at a height of 1–2 m (3–6½ ft) above the ground. Up to 20 m (66 ft) wide, they were covered with limestone plaster and often included ramps and junctions. One of these ancient highways stretches over 100 km (62 miles) from Cobá to Xahuna near Chichén Itzá. More than 50 *sacbes* have been discovered at Cobá, all originating at the central plaza and stretching out in four general directions.

ⓐ 50 km (31 miles) northwest of Tulum ⓑ 07.00–18.00 daily ⓘ Regular tours run from Cancún, Playa del Carmen and the Riviera Maya, combined with a trip to Tulum's ruins, and shopping

TEOTIHUACÁN

Those who opt for a few days in Mexico City (see page 89) will not want to miss this ethereal site, just 48 km (30 miles) northeast of the capital. Once the largest city in the Americas, Teotihuacán is considered by many to be the most important archaeological site in the world. At its height, the population of the city was greater than that of Rome. The city was built around the **Avenida de los Muertos** (Avenue of the Dead). The third-largest pyramid in the world is here – the imposing **Pirámide del Sol** (Pyramid of the Sun). At the other end is the **Pirámide de la Luna** (Pyramid of the Moon).

The area was occupied from around 500 BC for a thousand years, when it was abandoned. It was discovered six centuries later by the Aztecs. Because the city's founders did not leave a writing system, its origins and the true names of its features were never known. When the Aztecs established the site as a ceremonial ground, they gave the city its name, which means 'Place of the Gods'.

It was also the Aztecs who named the tallest structure the 'Pyramid of the Sun' because the front wall faces the exact point on the horizon where the sun sets at the spring and autumn equinoxes. This pyramid is 70 m (77 yds) high with a 220-m (241-yd) base. It was built around AD 150.

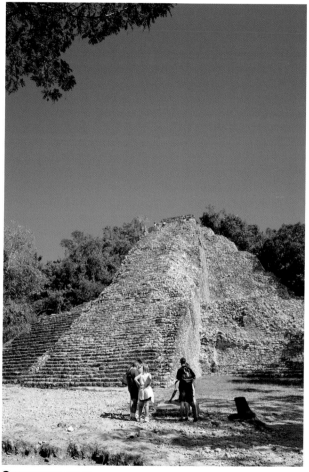

⬭ *Mayan ruins at Cobá*

> **A BITE TO EAT**
> Out at the pyramids in Teotihuacán, **La Gruta ££** is a restaurant in a natural grotto that makes a great place to round off a visit to the archaeological site. JFK dined here. ⓐ Zona Arqueológica Teotihuacán ⓘ 594 956 0127/0104 ⓛ Until 19.00 daily
> ⓘ Reservations recommended

The now neutral stone façade was originally painted bright red. The smaller Pyramid of the Moon was built between AD 250 and 600.

At the entrance to Teotihuacán, keep an eye out for groups of men in traditional costume gathering around a tall pole. These are the **Voladores de Papantla** (Papantla Flyers). They climb the pole, one perches on top playing a flute and four others 'fly' down the pole, spinning around it, and supported only by a rope from their ankle. The show is repeated several times daily and the team passes a hat around for tips afterwards. ⓐ Teotihuacán is about 48 km (30 miles) northwest of Mexico City – about an hour's drive. Buses leave from the capital's north bus terminal every 30–60 minutes ⓛ 09.00–17.00 Tues–Sun, closed Mon ⓘ Organised tours to Teotihuacán are available from Mexico City, either as part of a group on a bus or in a private car that will give you added flexibility during your trip; many hotels based in Mexico City also arrange local tours to the pyramids that include transportation, food and a guided tour.

TULUM
These Mayan ruins perched on a cliff top overlooking the Caribbean are certainly not Mexico's biggest, but are arguably the most beautifully located. The walled fortress was built to protect Tulum, one of the main ports of the Mayan civilisation. Don't miss the impressive tower, **El Castillo**, or **El Templo de los Frescos**. ⓐ 68 km (42 miles) south of Playa del Carmen ⓛ 08.00–17.00 daily ⓘ Full day trips from Cancún and the resorts of the Riviera Maya usually combine a visit to the ruins with entry to the aquatic theme park **Xel-Ha** (see page 83)

⬥ *Papantla Flyers are guaranteed to amaze onlookers*

Jungles, rivers & wildlife

Should you tire of life on the beach, the Yucatán is home to a host of nature reserves, parks and attractions that showcase the enormous biodiversity this country has to offer.

SIAN KA'AN BIOSPHERE RESERVE

This wildlife reserve near Tulum covers 528,000 hectares (1⅓ million acres) and includes rainforest, wetlands, savannas, mangroves and marine environments. A UNESCO World Heritage Site, the wildlife here ranges from tiny, colourful butterflies to families of howler monkeys, pumas and jaguars. Among the 330-plus bird species in the reserve is the jabiru stork – the world's largest bird capable of flight. A good-value all-day tour can be booked directly with the park administrator, **Centro Ecológico Sian Ka'an** (Ⓦ www.cesiak.org), which combines walking, swimming and boat travel through the lagoons in the reserve.

It's free to drive through the reserve, but, to get the most out of it, call **Friends of Sian Ka'an** (Ⓣ 998 884 9583) to book a guided tour. They are a non-profit organisation, so the money they receive is ploughed back into the reserve.

If you are staying in Playa del Carmen or Cancún, your guide will normally pick you up from your hotel. If you are coming from further afield, or want to spend more time in the reserve, you can book into the comfortable, on-site visitor centre. Alternatively, inclusive week-long tours with airport pick-up are offered by **Ecocolors** (Ⓣ 998 884 3667 Ⓦ www.ecotravelmexico.com).

ⓐ The reserve itself is situated three hours south of Cancún, past Tulum, on the road to Boca Paila and Punta Allen Ⓛ 09.00–21.00 daily

XCARET

An hour's drive from Cancún, this natural wonder has been transformed into a popular theme park, with snorkelling and swimming tours through underground rivers as well as dolphin programmes, and spectacular evening shows that hark back to the glory days of the

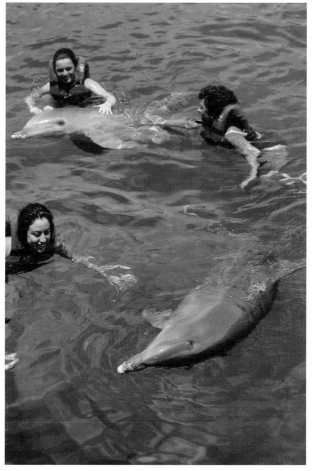

⬤ *Swimming with dolphins at Xcaret*

Maya. Don't miss the chance to see a tapir – a strange and rare beast that looks like a cross between a pig and an anteater. You might even catch a glimpse of the big cats that roam around 'Jaguar Island'. You can arrange to be picked up from your hotel, and the cost will be added to the price of your ticket, which is a rather astronomical US$69 (at time of publishing) per person. Tickets purchased online will receive a 10 per cent discount. Visit the **Xcaret Information Center** in Cancún's Hotel Zone (ⓐ Next to the Fiesta Americana Grand Coral Ⓦ www.xcaret.com). A cheaper alternative is to get there by bus and pay on entry. Take a bus from your resort to Playa del Carmen. From Playa del Carmen, it's a short taxi ride, or you can take one of the many buses. ⓐ Xcaret is about 70 km (43 miles) from Cancún, close to Playa del Carmen ❶ 998 883 0470 Ⓦ www.xcaret.com ● 08.30–22.00 daily

▲ *A panoramic view of Xel-Ha*

XEL-HA

A group of coves, lagoons, rivers and mangroves make up this eco theme park, where you can get close to nature. Swim with tropical fish in crystal-clear rivers, snorkel through the underwater caves or just hop on one of the free bicycles and explore. When it's time to relax, retreat to the beach, the spa or one of the many restaurants in the complex. Although a trip to the park is often combined with a visit to the ruins in Tulum, there is plenty to keep you occupied here for a full day.

ⓐ Xel-Ha is 121 km (75 miles) south of Cancún ⓦ www.xelha.com
ⓛ 08.30–18.00 daily ⓘ If you are travelling by bus (they run frequently from the downtown bus station in Cancún and along the coast), take a bus towards Tulum and ask the driver to let you off at the road near the park entrance, which is about a 2-km (1¼-mile) walk away.

Colonial history

A trip to one of the Yucatán's old colonial cities or towns makes a pleasant change from the hectic pace of the larger coastal resorts. The people tend to be friendlier, the atmosphere is more authentic and you will have more time to get under the skin of the real Mexico, as well as discovering more of its complex past.

MÉRIDA

The state capital of the Yucatán was built on the ashes of the Mayan city T'ho. Once the Spanish had triumphed, they tore down the pyramids and built the **Catedral de San Idelfonso**, the oldest cathedral on the North American continent. Today, Mérida is a bustling city of around 750,000 people and the peninsula's cultural centre. Either wander around its charming narrow streets and colonial buildings, or go on a short bus or horse-drawn carriage tour to take in the city's lovely gardens and plazas. There are lots of hotels and restaurants of every class and price range and good transport available to any part of the peninsula. Mérida is busiest with tourists in July and August, when it is also very humid. Winter is a more pleasant, cooler time to visit.

ⓐ Mérida is around a five-hour drive from both Cancún and Tulum

ⓘ There are plenty of sightseeing trips available from Mérida, including some less visited archaeological sites

VALLADOLID

Pronounced 'Bah-yah-doh-leeth', this is a pleasant colonial town halfway between Mérida and Cancún. Founded in 1552, the town boasts the convent of **San Bernardino de Siena**, one of the most beautiful buildings of the colonial era. The **Cenote Dzinup**, south of the town, is a marvellous underground well with stalactites and vines, making for a spooky atmosphere, and you can swim in it, too. The **Cenote Zaci** in the town centre is popular for swimming and snorkelling, as it is inhabited by a rare species of eyeless black fish known as a 'lub'.

ⓐ Valladolid is 40 km (25 miles) east of Chichén Itzá, between Mérida and Cancún, with regular buses departing from both places ❶ If you are driving, it is quicker via the toll road, but Carretera 180 winds through a number of scenic villages

⬣ *Mérida's Catedral de San Idelfonso*

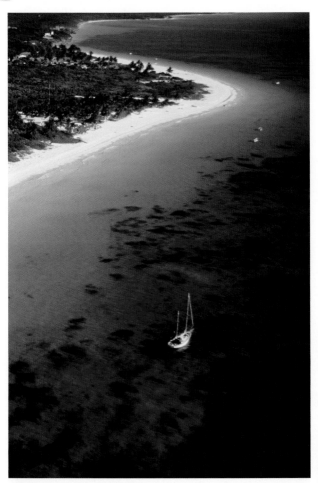

⬭ *See the Riviera Maya from the air*

Air tours

The Mexican novelist Carlos Fuentes said: 'To see Mexico from the air is to look upon the face of creation.' From the sky, you will get a unique view of the wonders of the Yucatán, whether soaring over the Caribbean islands or spotting Mayan ruins in the depths of the jungle.

PANORAMIC FLIGHTS
Mangroves, beaches & Cozumel

Atlas Sky Tours offers short flights in an ultralight aircraft. You and your pilot will fly low over the mangroves and beaches on the coast, and take in the island of Cozumel. ⓐ Next to the Xcaret eco-park ⓣ 984 871 4020 ⓘ Flights last 20–30 minutes

Playa del Carmen & the Caribbean Sea

From Playa del Carmen, you can take a flight that gives you a bird's-eye view of the coast and a panoramic view of Playa del Carmen and the Caribbean Sea. Flights with **Aerosaab** last for 30 minutes, 45 minutes or 1 hour and prices range from about US$583 to US$748 per person. ⓐ Avenida 20 Sur and Calle 1, next to Playa del Carmen Airport ⓣ 984 873 0804 ⓦ www.aerosaab.com ⓛ 07.00–19.30 daily ⓘ Flights do not include tax; an additional 10 per cent sales tax applies on each ticket

Holbox Island

This tiny island northwest of Cancún is just 42 km (26 miles) long. It is separated from the mainland of Mexico by a shallow lagoon, which forms a sanctuary for thousands of flamingos, pelicans and exotic birds. Holbox is essentially a fishing community, where the streets are sand and cars are uncommon. The island's inaccessibility means it has so far been protected from mass tourism and its natural beauty has been largely unspoilt.

Flights to Holbox can easily be arranged from Playa del Carmen and Cancún. The trip takes in panoramic views of the Riviera Maya and Isla Mujeres. Tours include a boat trip to the even smaller **Isla Pájaros** (Island

of the Birds), where thousands of flamingos and other birds feed. Other natural attractions include iguanas, horseshoe crabs and a wonderful array of wild plants. You may even be lucky to catch sight of dolphins swimming in the sheltered waters. Tours also include a fresh fish lunch, a visit to a mandolin factory and a walk around the main village.

Aerosaab (see page 87 for details) runs day trips three times a week from Playa del Carmen. ❶ Bring your swimming costume, sunscreen and a towel, and wear comfortable shoes

PRIVATE CHARTER FLIGHTS

Aerosaab (see page 87) offers private charter tours to many parts of the Yucatán Peninsula, including Mérida and the Uxmal ruins, Cancún and Isla Mujeres, and various other combinations. Its Cessna planes can accommodate four or five people for $350 from Cancún to Playa del Carmen, $460 from Cancún to Cozumel and $895 from Cancún to Chichén Itzá an hour at the time of writing. Rather than travel by bus for several hours, why not fly to Chichén Itzá in under an hour from Playa del Carmen, Cancún or Cozumel? This way you can get to these sights by mid-morning and avoid the crowds and the heat of the sun.

Mexico City

Mexico City is a holiday destination in itself, but many visitors choose to spend a couple of days here before heading to one of the coastal resorts, or to break their stay on the beach with a two-day tour. As the ancient centre of the Aztec empire, the city was called Tenochtitlán, and was built on an island in the middle of Lake Toxcoco. After the Spanish defeated the Aztecs, they drained the lake, but the spectacular canals and 'Floating Gardens' of Xochimilco (see below) still remain.

THINGS TO SEE & DO

In the centre, the city is much like a grand European capital, with wide boulevards and large public buildings. The *zócalo*, officially known as the **Plaza de la Constitución**, is the hub of Mexico City. This massive public square was laid out in 1529 as a testament to Spanish power in the New World, and grand buildings surround it on all sides. The **Palacio Nacional**, on the eastern side of the plaza, is the seat of the Mexican government and features murals by Diego Rivera.

Bosque de Chapultepec

This large park is the city's lungs, and offers a welcome respite if the pollution gets too much for you. At weekends, the city's families flock here. The grand castle that was once the residence of Emperor Maximilian is worth a look.

Floating Gardens of Xochimilco

In the south of the city is this large network of canals and islands, centred around the historic neighbourhood of Xochimilco. Visitors can hire one of the decorated boats, rather like Venice's gondolas, and enjoy a leisurely afternoon cruise. At the weekend, the place is packed with locals, many of whom bring their lunch to eat in the boats. *Mariachi* musicians who board the *trajineras* (as the boats are known) add to the atmosphere.

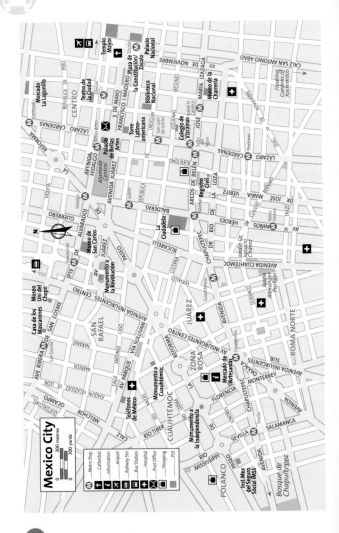

Mexico City

SHOPPING

You'll find plenty to buy in this city, much of it from all over Mexico. For clothes, antiques, art and much more wander around the Zona Rosa. In this area you'll also find a branch of **Fonart** (ⓐ Londres 136A Ⓦ www.fonart.gob.mx), a government-supported organisation with shops throughout the country that sell quality handicrafts such as glassware, wall hangings and ceramics. No bargaining is allowed because the government sets the prices, but they are reasonable.

A little more than 1 km (½ mile) south of the Alameda Central is La Ciudadela (The Citadel), an area where people come to shop at the nearby **Centro Artesanías La Ciudadela** and at the **open-air market** at the Plaza del Buen Tono. These two places sell handicrafts from all over Mexico, at prices that are fair even before you begin bargaining.

North of Bosque de Chapultepec, **Polanco** is a swish shopping district packed with fashionable boutiques, cigar emporiums, jewellers and leather-goods stores. If you're looking for fine crafts, antiques and collectibles, try the **Bazar de la Roma** in Colonia Roma. More trinkety objects are available at the **Bazar Artesanal de Coyoacán**.

Templo Mayor

Spanish colonial buildings were demolished in order to excavate the Templo Mayor, which was constructed by the Aztecs in 1325. Little remains of the pyramid that dominated what is now Plaza Templo Mayor and artefacts that have been excavated thus far are housed inside the museum, which has eight halls exhibiting a wealth of objects that provide an engaging and rather brutal insight into Aztec rule.

Museo del Templo Mayor ⓐ Calle Seminario 8, Centro Histórico
🕒 09.00–17.00 Tues–Sun, closed Mon

Torre Latinoamericana

Take in sublime views of Mexico City from the top floor of this 44-storey skyscraper, four blocks west of the *zócalo*. There is an aquarium on the 38th floor (supposedly the world's highest!) and viewing platforms above.

ⓐ Avenida Madero and Lázaro Cárdenas, Centro Histórico

🕒 10.00–23.00 daily

A BITE TO EAT

Arrive early at **La Nueva Opera** to enjoy great Mexican food at reasonable prices while you soak up the atmosphere in a comfortable booth. Legend has it that Pancho Villa rode in on his horse and fired his gun at the ceiling – you can still see the bullet hole (ⓐ Cinco de Mayo 10, Alameda 🕒 Closed Sun night). Classic Mexican dishes are infused with a modern aesthetic at the minimalist **Izote** in the gilded enclosure of Polanco. Chef and TV personality Patricia Quintana is a local institution, so reservations are always essential (ⓐ Presidente Masasyk 513 ☎ 55 5280 1265 ❶ Lunch only on Sun). Modern Mexican gastronomy reaches its zenith at **Aguila y Sol**, a chi-chi restaurant that is owned by famous Mexican food writer Marta Ortiz Chapa (ⓐ Emilio Castelar 229 ☎ 55 5281 8354 ❶ Reservations essential).

The city's cantinas are no longer for men only, and the atmosphere in **Cantina La Guadalupana** is welcoming and fun. Open since 1928 and steeped in history, this is a great place to enjoy a beer and tapas (ⓐ Higuera 14, Coyoacán 🕒 Mon–Sat, closed Sun). Sanborn's **Casa de Azulejos** is a beautiful building with a façade of elaborate stonemasonry and mosaic tiles. Eat in the courtyard and admire the architecture, or go upstairs for a cosy drink and meal (ⓐ Opposite the Torre Latinoamericana).

▶ *Religion and music, both play important roles in Mexican culture*

LIFESTYLE
Mexican life

Food & drink

Mexican cuisine is one of the most exciting and creative you can find anywhere. Reflecting the country's history, it is a blend of the Old and New Worlds. Pre-Columbian influences mean local ingredients such as tomatoes, corn and chilli are used, while the use of chicken, beef, onions and garlic is a result of the country's Spanish and French heritage.

Expect to tuck into much more than just tacos and refried beans. You can enjoy a wide variety of fruit and vegetables, great steaks and delicious fish and seafood. In tourist areas international food is easy to find, but vegetarians may have a hard time.

There are more than 100 different types of chilli, and not all of them are hot. Mexican dishes are not necessarily spicy, and you can always order them *sin chile* (without chilli).

MEAL TIMES

Mexicans eat at any time of the day, and food is nearly always on offer from street stalls. Locals will often have two breakfasts. The first, a snack of fruit and bread, is eaten at home, followed by a meal at 10.00 or 11.00 of eggs and tortillas. Lunch, served from around 13.30, is usually the main meal of the day and can continue for several hours. Snacks are often eaten between 18.00 and 20.00, followed by a light dinner, although restaurants serve big meals in the evening.

TYPES OF RESTAURANT

Most of the large hotels serve buffet evening meals, and many have a selection of restaurants serving different cuisines. *Fondas* are good-value, family-run restaurants with fixed lunch menus that are usually a real bargain. Visit a *cantina* to eat in a bar-style atmosphere. Mexicans like to eat accompanied by music, and many larger restaurants have a live band performing at least once a week.

⬤ *A Mexico City street food vendor*

MEXICAN DISHES

Mexicans eat tortillas like we eat bread. These corn pancakes are stuffed, rolled up and toasted or baked to make *enchiladas*, *tostadas*, tacos or *quesadillas*. *Frijoles* (beans) are eaten with just about everything and are usually mashed, refried or served whole in stews or soups. *Chiles en nogada* is the national dish, symbolising Mexican independence and available only between August and October. It is made with poblano chillies (spicy green peppers) stuffed with meat and covered in a white cream sauce and red pomegranate seeds – the three colours representing the Mexican flag.

DRINKS

Tequila, distilled from the blue agave plant, is Mexico's national drink and enjoyed all over the world. Drink it straight as a shot, or in a Margarita or Tequila Sunrise cocktail. Gold tequila is not necessarily of superior quality, and often has colourings, and even flavourings, added. Consult the locals if you want to try the best tequila. Mezcal can be made from a number of varieties of agave and often includes a worm as decoration and flavouring. Tequila is never served with a worm. Kahlúa is a Mexican coffee-based liqueur that forms the basis of a Black Russian.

Mexican *cervezas* (beers) are excellent and come in three varieties: *clara* (light), *campechana* (medium) and *oscura* (dark). Corona and Sol are two of the lighter brews; Superior, Bohemia and Dos Equis are somewhat heavier. Mexicans aren't big wine drinkers, but you can find international labels, and local wines are usually reasonable. *Jugos* (fresh juices) are a delicious and healthy option.

Menu decoder

Common terms & dishes

A la plancha Grilled

Al mojo de ajo With garlic sauce

Antojitos Meaning something close to little cravings, these bite-sized little appetisers are on sale everywhere, from street booths and wandering vendors to *cantinas*. Meant to be eaten informally, most are made from fried corn dough filled with cheese but they can also appear as soups or stuffed jalapeños

Barbacoa Lamb cooked in a pot

Caldo largo Soup of fish and seafood

Ceviche Raw fish marinated in lime juice, often in a chopped salad

Crepa Crêpe, usually with a savoury filling

Flan Crème caramel

Frijoles Beans, often refried

Huevos rancheros Fried eggs

○ *Tequila is Mexico's national drink*

on fried tortillas with tomato sauce

Menú del día Set menu

Mole Sauce made with dark chocolate, chillies and spices

Pan Bread

Pescado a la Veracruzana Red snapper with a tomato, olive and caper sauce

Picante Spicy

Pollo al pibil Steamed chicken with *achiote*, a local seasoning

Postre Dessert

Queso Cheese

Salsas Sauces usually made with raw vegetables or tomato and chillies

Sopa Soup

Sopa Azteca Tomato soup with fried tortillas, avocado and sour cream

Taco Soft or crisp fried tortilla, filled with meat, seafood, beans or cheese

Tamales Steamed corn dumplings with meat and chillies, wrapped in corn husks or banana leaves

Torta Large sandwich, served hot

Tortilla Omelette

Tortillas Thin, round pancakes of corn or wheat

Tostadas Thin and crispy tortillas served loaded with guacamole, sour cream, chillies, chicken etc

Meat & seafood

Almejas Clams

Calamares Squid

Camarones Prawns

Cangrejo Crab

Carne Meat, usually beef

Cerdo Pork

Chorizo Spicy pork sausage

Cordero Lamb

Langosta Lobster

Mariscos Shellfish

Mejillones Mussels

Pato Duck

Pavo Turkey

Pescado Fish

Pollo Chicken

Pulpo Octopus

Tocino Bacon

Fruit & vegetables

Aguacate Avocado

Coco Coconut

Ensalada Salad

Frijoles Beans

Fruta Fruit

Papa Potato

Verduras Vegetables

Shopping

Shopping can be one of the highlights of a Mexican holiday. Everything from traditional handicrafts to contemporary silver jewellery is on offer, whether from the many local markets or designer boutiques.

BARGAINING

Bargaining in Mexico can be viewed as a dance between the two parties – there are very strict moves and it should be enjoyed. Always be polite and good-humoured about the procedure and start to bargain only if you intend to buy the item – breaking off negotiations can be a long process! Decide what you want to pay and ask the seller for the price. Then offer about half of what you want to pay. He or she will more than likely drop the price and then hopefully you can raise your offer to the price you want. If you walk away and sellers know they are asking too much, they will probably call you back to renegotiate.

ARTS & CRAFTS

Indigenous art and handicrafts are best bought directly from the artisans and workshops that produce them. Reproductions of traditional masks are good buys, as are hand-woven cotton or wool wall hangings and rugs. *Calaveras*, little skeleton figures used as part of the Day of the Dead festival (see page 106), make great presents, and everywhere you go you will see *muñecas* (handmade dolls).

Keep an eye out for unusual *nacimientos* (Nativity-scene Christmas decorations) made of coloured tin, clay or wood. Semi-precious stones can be found in many shops, with Mexican amber considered the best in the world. Mexico's official handicraft shops, **Fonart**, stock a wonderful variety of goods from all over the country. This organisation ploughs back profits into supporting arts and crafts throughout Mexico.

CLOTHING

Guayaberas are traditional shirts worn by Mexican men and boys. Usually white and made of cotton and linen, they are often intricately embroidered. *Huipiles* are the female version. A *jorongo* is a wool or cotton rectangular poncho that is a very practical way of staying warm. *Rebozos* are traditional woven shawls, made of cotton or silk and often featuring beautiful designs.

LEATHER GOODS

Leather shoes and accessories are usually of good quality in Mexico and much cheaper than at home. Look for boots and shoes found in many colours, styles and skins, which can usually be made to measure for a reasonable price. Handbags and wallets are good buys as well.

⬤ *Handicrafts such as woven baskets and rugs make a good buy*

Children

Mexicans love children, and yours will be welcome everywhere that you are. Many of the larger resort hotels have kids' clubs, pools and activities for youngsters, as well as babysitting services. On the beach, entertainment comes in the form of swimming, watersports and beach activities. If you venture further afield, there will still be plenty to keep your offspring amused.

If you are travelling with young children, then anywhere from Cancún to Playa del Carmen and all along the Riviera Maya is good to visit. The northern tip of Cancún has the safest beaches because Isla Mujeres blocks the currents there, but there are safe beaches with lifeguards on duty at the other resorts, too. The main strip, Avenida 5, in Playa del Carmen (see page 40) is a great place for older children and teens to shop for clothes and have their hair braided.

ALL THE FUN OF THE FAIR

If you visit the capital, Mexico City, consider taking the children to **Feria de Chapultepec**. This funfair has more than 50 rides, including a wooden roller coaster from the 1960s. The day passes are good value.

THEME PARKS

Forty-five minutes from Cancún is **Xcaret Eco Theme Park**, great fun for adults as well as children. On offer is an aquarium, butterfly pavilion, lagoons and a 'Swim with Dolphins Tour'. ❶ 998 883 0470 Ⓦ www.xcaret.com

WILDLIFE

Mexico teems with wildlife that will excite most children. In Cozumel (see page 58), Isla Mujeres (see page 25) and Puerto Aventuras (see page 49), give them the opportunity to swim with dolphins with **Dolphin Discovery**. Ⓦ www.dolphindiscovery.com ❶ Children must be eight years or older

WATER PARKS

Wet'n Wild is the only water park in the Riviera Maya. Located in Cancún's Hotel Zone it has 244 m (267 yds) of white sand beach and lots of activities for all ages. Parents can relax on the 'Lazy River', and there's also a wave pool, children's playground and 'kamikaze' ride for thrill-seeking teenagers, plus three bars and a large restaurant. Lockers, towels and inner tubes to rent.

ⓐ Parque Nizuc, Cancún ❶ 998 881 3000 ⓦ www.wetnwildcancun.com

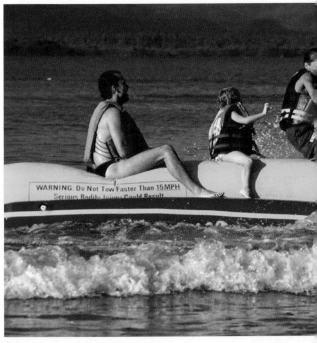

WARNING: Do Not Tow Faster Than 15MPH
Serious Bodily Injury Could Result

🔺 *Making waves on a banana boat*

WATERSPORTS

Most children can't resist the water, whether it is paddling in the sea or taking a boat trip, and there are lots of opportunities for both in this part of Mexico. **Aquaworld** is Cancún's largest watersports centre, offering plenty of options, including a trip on the 'Subsee Explorer', on which children can explore the coral reef in a glass-bottomed boat.

ⓐ Boulevard Kukulcán Km 15.2, Cancún ⓣ 998 848 8300
ⓦ www.aquaworld.com.mx ⓔ info@aquaworld.com.mx

Sports & activities

The Yucatán, with its vast stretches of coastline and warm climate, offers plenty of opportunities for watersports. The beaches on the Caribbean coast are generally calm and safe, but take heed of local warnings: beneath the apparently calm surf lurk dangerous undertows. Most of the popular beaches rent watersports equipment, whether you are looking for a gentle trip around the bay in a pedalo or a thrilling ride on waterskis. Opportunities for sailing and boat rides abound, with modern marinas dotted around the coast.

DIVING & SNORKELLING

Mexico has some of the best diving sites to be found anywhere, and the Yucatán boasts the world's second-largest coral reef, parts of which were made famous by Jacques Cousteau. Calm waters allow for excellent visibility, and facilities are mostly of a good standard.

The Caribbean Sea has visibility of 15–45 m (50–150 ft) and wonderfully warm waters that rarely drop below 21°C (70°F). Around Cancún (see page 15), there are a dozen excellent diving sites, many of which are conveniently located near the larger hotels.

The island of Isla Mujeres (see page 25) features dive sites such as the '**Cave of the Sleeping Sharks**', where close encounters with sharks can be had, and **Garrafón Natural Reef Park**, with good visitor facilities. The island of Cozumel (see page 58) alone has more than 100 dive sites, many of which are shallow enough for snorkelling. Divers can explore plunging walls, underwater caverns, swimming among rare coral, giant sponges and an incredible variety of tropical fish – no fewer than 250 species. At the **Chankanaab Park** on Cozumel, there is a lagoon that is perfect for beginners.

The Riviera Maya is dotted with good snorkelling sites and you can rent snorkelling equipment from all the upmarket hotels. Popular locations include the resort of Playa del Carmen (see page 40), **Xcaret Eco Theme Park** (see page 80), Akumal and the reserve of **Xel-Ha** (see page 83) with its fresh springs. Further south again is the World Heritage Site

of **Sian Ka'an Biosphere Reserve** (see page 80) and a 96-km (60-mile) chain of coral reefs. *Cenote* and cave diving are both very popular, but only for the experienced.

FISHING

Some of the best deep-sea fishing in the world is found off the Caribbean coast. Tuna, sea bass and swordfish are all common catches. All of the resorts featured in this book are home to operators who can arrange fishing trips, for just a few hours, or for a few weeks.

GOLF

Mexico is a fast-growing golf destination, thanks partly to its beautiful and diverse scenery, and Cancún is now one of the country's top golfing centres. Cancún's oldest course is located at **Club de Golf Cancún**. The 18 holes have views of the sea and lagoon, and there are also tennis courts and a swimming pool (ⓐ Boulevard Kukulcán Km 7.5 ⓘ 998 883 1230 ⓦ www.cancungolfclub.com). The **Hilton Cancún Golf & Spa Resort** (see page 17) is another popular course, although green fees can be very expensive.

🔺 *The Yucatán's clear, warm waters entice many to snorkelling and scuba diving*

Festivals & events

Many of Mexico's celebrations are regional affairs and are often based around a religious event; many celebrate local patron saints. You will find small fairs and harvest festivals taking place year-round, but there are also several big, national events. There's Carnaval, of course – the third largest in the world after Rio and New Orleans – as well as Easter (which constitutes Holy Week, or Semana Santa), Independence Day, the Day of the Dead, the Feast of the Virgin of Guadalupe and Christmas, which are all celebrated throughout the country with wholehearted festivity. Check the date of celebrations, particularly Easter and Carnaval, as they may vary by a few days from year to year.

THE DAY OF THE DEAD
One of Mexico's most unusual celebrations is the Day of the Dead (*el Día de los Muertos*), which takes place on 2 November, also known as All Souls' Day (the lead-up to this is All Saints' Day, on 1 November). You may be surprised to learn that this is not a macabre event, but is when Mexicans remember their dead loved ones, bringing presents of food, candles and incense to their graveside in the belief that their spirit will return on this day. Skulls and skeletons made out of sugar, papier-mâché and other materials can be seen in the shops, and special bread is made.

THE FEAST OF THE VIRGIN OF GUADALUPE
This huge, nationwide event – and one of Mexico's most important expressions of traditional culture – is held to honour the country's patron saint, said to have appeared to a young man called Juan Diego in 1531 on a hill near Mexico City. A traditional 'Happy Birthday' song is sung at dawn, and there are special church services, followed by dancing and fireworks. Celebrations start on 1 December and carry on through to 12 December, with local variations, depending on where you are.

🔺 *The Day of the Dead is a vibrant celebration, and far from morbid*

CALENDAR OF EVENTS

January

6 January	**Three Kings Day** commemorates the Three Kings bringing gifts to Jesus. Children are given presents, and a special cake is eaten.

February

2 February	**Candlemas** marks the end of winter with parties at home and in the street.
5 February	Street festivities on **Constitution Day** celebrate the signing of the Mexican constitution in 1917.
Week before Lent	**Carnaval** is an exuberant, five-day festival that sometimes falls in March.

March

21 March	**Benito Juárez's Birthday** is a national holiday in honour of the impoverished Zapotec Indian who became one of Mexico's most-loved presidents.

April

Palm Sunday–Easter Sunday	**Holy Week**, which includes Easter, with religious processions. The country's biggest holiday period.

May

1 May	**Labour Day** is a national holiday.
5 May	**Cinco de Mayo** commemorates the Battle of Puebla in 1862, when the Mexicans successfully fought off the invading French army.

June

1 June	**Navy Day** is honoured in coastal towns by naval parades and fireworks.
29 June	**St Peter's and St Paul's Day** is observed in various locations.

🔺 *Independence Day* matraces *(rattles)*

August

13 August   **The Fall of Tenochtitlán** commemorates the last battle of the Spanish Conquest and the surrender of the last Aztec king to Hernán Cortés in 1521. The loss of thousands of lives is remembered in wreath-laying ceremonies in Mexico City.

15 August   **The Feast of the Assumption** is celebrated by religious processions.

September

15–16 September   **Independence Day** is an important national holiday that celebrates Mexico's independence from Spain in 1810 with parades and parties.

October

12 October   **El Día de la Raza** originally celebrated Columbus arriving in the Americas, but now honours the ancient Mexicans.

November

1–2 November   **The Day of the Dead** is a national holiday that continues for two days and includes All Saints' Day and All Souls' Day (see page 106).

20 November   **Revolution Day** is a national holiday that commemorates the start of the Mexican Revolution in 1910. The day is filled with parades, speeches, rodeos and patriotic events.

December

12 December   **The Feast of the Virgin of Guadalupe** (see page 106).

16–24 December   **Posadas** celebrates Mary and Joseph's search for a lodging, with door-to-door candlelight processions.

▶ *A stop sign in Isla Mujeres*

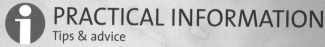

PRACTICAL INFORMATION
Tips & advice

Accommodation

£ = under £50   ££ = £50–100   £££ = over £100

CANCÚN

J W Marriott £££ There is nothing minimalist about this luxurious Caribbean theme enclave. Guest rooms drip with marble and every conceivable convenience is lavished with aplomb by the super-efficient staff. The infinity pool fuses with the shimmering ocean, and with a fantastic kids' club, there is still plenty of opportunity for soulful sunworshipping and romance. ⓐ Boulevard Kukulcán Km 14.5 ⓣ 998 848 9600 ⓦ www.marriott.com

ISLA MUJERES

Na Balam £££ Rustic chic reaches its zenith in this idyllic beachside hotel with individually designed *palapa* rooms that conjure feelings of natural exoticism without sacrificing creature comforts. A Mayan theme fused with Eastern philosophy prevails in the artwork, food and on-site activities, which include meditation, massage and yoga. ⓐ Calle Zazil-Ha 118 ⓣ 998 877 0446 ⓦ www.nabalam.com

PUERTO MORELOS

Ceiba del Mar Beach & Spa Resort ££ A tropical theme combines with discreet service and charming rustic bedrooms at this off-the-beaten track, artistic retreat, which is a world apart from the monolithic hotels at the larger resorts. In each bedroom, mosaic tiles and locally crafted hardwood furnishings provide a relaxing backdrop for the stunning sea views. ⓐ Avenida Niños Héroes ⓣ 998 872 8060 ⓦ www.ceibadelmar.com

PLAYA DEL CARMEN & PLAYACAR

Deseo Hotel + Lounge ££ Minimalist and cool, with more than a whiff of pretension, this contemporary hotel transforms an otherwise banal, nondescript building into one of the hippest spots in town. The rooftop deck complete with beds draped with white curtains, a cocktail bar and a swimming pool is the major draw. ❸ Avenida 5 and Calle 12 ❶ 984 879 3620 Ⓦ www.hoteldeseo.com ❶ No children

PUERTO AVENTURAS

Aventura Spa Palace £££ There is nothing restrained about this beautiful, well-conceived all-inclusive resort with a palatial lobby, dazzling rooms and an indulgent ambience. The entertainment and amenities at this hacienda-style complex are myriad, from a fully equipped gym, tennis courts, spa, six restaurants and several swimming pools complete with waterfalls, and even a cross-current marine pool. ❸ Carretera Cancún-Chetumal Km 72 ❶ 435 627 0503 Ⓦ www.palaceresorts.com

COZUMEL

Presidente InterContinental Cozumel Resort & Spa £££ Offers elegant, modern rooms with spacious bathrooms and unrivalled guest convenience in the abundance of on-site activities and amenities. ❸ Carretera Chankanaab Km 6.5 ❶ 987 872 9500 Ⓦ www.interconti.com

AKUMAL

Villa Las Brisas £ This pleasant, attractively decorated white stucco villa, set amid a beautiful tropical garden and complete with a fully equipped kitchen and a spacious sitting area, provides an excellent family base for a relaxing beachside holiday. The owners are extremely friendly and helpful, and the price is hard to beat. ❸ At Akumal's southernmost point, around 3 km (2 miles) south of the sign for Playa Akumal ❶ 984 876 2110 Ⓦ www.aventuras-akumal.com

MEXICO CITY

Hotel Marquis Reforma £££ This business-orientated boutique hotel constantly makes Mexico City's 'best of' lists, and for service, style and location it is worthy of the hype. Despite its appeal to business travellers, the overall ambience is cosy, relaxed and artistic. ❸ Paseo de la Reforma 465 ❶ 55 5229 1200 Ⓦ www.marquisreforma.com

Preparing to go

GETTING THERE

There are plenty of tour operators offering package holidays to the Yucatán. Most people pop into their local travel agent and start flicking through brochures of the popular resorts, and this is often the best way to find a package you like. Travel agents often have insider knowledge about certain hotels, and this can be very useful. An exhaustive list of tour operators is given on the UK version of the Mexico Tourism Board's website (Ⓦ www.visitmexico.com). The Latin American Travel Association (LATA) provides extensive information on Mexican culture as well as informative travel resources (Ⓦ www.lata.org). If you are looking for something out of the ordinary, perhaps a longer and more varied itinerary than usual, then it's a good idea to speak to a specialist travel agent. **Journey Latin America** (Ⓣ 020 8747 8315 Ⓦ www.journeylatinamerica.co.uk) and **Trailfinders** (Ⓣ 020 7938 3939 Ⓦ www.trailfinders.com) are highly rated.

SWINE FLU OUTBREAK

The H1N1 (swine flu) virus was first detected in April 2009 in Mexico and rapidly became a global pandemic. In Mexico alone, 610 lives were lost between April and November, and more than 65,000 people were infected. As of January 2010, a huge government-led vaccination programme had begun to be administered and swine fatalities dwindled away to pre-pandemic levels.

Following the outbreak, the tourist industry (which represents 88 per cent of Mexico's gross national product) imploded, with economists predicting that the crisis would take 0.8 per cent off Mexico's GDP if visitor numbers didn't return to normal levels by 2010. With Mexico already in the grip of a violent drug war and the continuing fallout from the global recession, the future looks uncertain.

By air

You can fly direct from Europe to Mexico City and Cancún. British Airways (☎ 0870 850 9850 Ⓦ www.ba.com) flies non-stop from Heathrow to Mexico City, and the journey takes around 12 hours. Other carriers operating direct flights to Mexico City from Europe (but not London) include Air France (☎ 0870 142 4343 Ⓦ www.airfrance.com), Lufthansa (☎ 0845 7737 747 Ⓦ www.lufthansa.com) and Spain's national carrier, Iberia (☎ 0845 601 2854 Ⓦ www.iberia.com). An alternative is to fly with one of the US airlines such as American Airlines (☎ 800 904 6000 Ⓦ www.aa.com), and this usually involves a stop or change at somewhere like Miami or Dallas. However, getting through US customs can be a real chore, so think long and hard before choosing this option.

Many people are aware that air travel emits CO_2, which contributes to climate change. You may be interested in the possibility of lessening the environmental impact of your flight through the charity Climate Care, which offsets your CO_2 by funding environmental projects around the world. Visit Ⓦ www.jpmorganclimatecare.com

BEFORE YOU LEAVE

No particular inoculations are recommended for Mexico, but check with the Department of Health (Ⓦ www.dh.gov.uk) or the World Health Organization (Ⓦ www.who.int/en) for the latest information. In any case, it is always a good idea to be up to date on your tetanus, typhoid and polio immunisations. Malaria and dengue fever can be a problem, but this is only in certain rural regions that very few tourists are likely to visit.

If you are taking prescription medicines, ensure that you have enough for the duration of your visit, and an extra copy of the information sheet in case of loss. Note, however, that you may find it impossible to obtain the same medicines in Mexico. It is also worth having a dental check-up before you leave the UK.

A small first-aid kit can bring peace of mind, especially if you have small children. Consider including painkillers, plasters, antiseptic cream, travel sickness tablets and a remedy for upset stomachs. Repellent and light, long-sleeved clothing can give protection from mosquitoes. It is a good idea to take suntan lotion with you, because the factor number system is not always as reliable in Mexico as it is in the UK. Bear in mind that if you are not fussy about brands most toiletries are considerably cheaper than in the UK. Nappies and moisturising creams are available, but you might want to take some with you. The often-intense heat should not be underestimated: use plenty of sunscreen, wear a hat and take cover in the heat of the day.

ENTRY FORMALITIES

The most important documents you will need are your tickets and your passport. Check well in advance that your passport is up to date and it must be valid for at least six months. All children, including newborn babies, need their own passport now. It generally takes at least three weeks to process a passport renewal. This can be longer in the run-up to the summer months. Contact the **Passport Agency** for the latest information on how to renew your passport and the processing times involved (**❶** 0870 521 0410 **Ⓦ** www.ips.gov.uk).

As police do occasionally ask foreigners for ID, it is a good idea to take a photocopy of your passport to keep with you when you are out and about. Make sure the details of your plane tickets are correct well in advance. If you do think you might want to drive, take your driving licence, along with the licence of anybody else who intends to drive. By law, you must always carry your licence while driving in Mexico.

MONEY

You will need some currency before you go, especially if your flight gets you to your destination at the weekend or late in the day after the banks have closed. You can exchange money at the airport before you depart.

Once you arrive, you will find cash dispensers in all the resorts. Just look for the round blue Cirrus sign to use your cash card, or for the MasterCard or Visa logo to withdraw money from a credit card account. However, if you are planning to visit a quiet beach or a small mountain village, make sure you have enough cash to at least buy something to eat, and to get a taxi back to your hotel in an emergency.

CLIMATE

The Yucatán's beach resorts are usually hot and humid the whole year round, but from June to August temperatures can be unbearable. There is a chance of rain throughout the year, and the hurricane season runs from June to November.

BAGGAGE ALLOWANCE

Each fare-paying passenger is allowed to carry a certain amount of baggage. However, how much baggage you are allowed and how much you have to pay for extra items and additional weight differs depending on your destination.

There are two systems that airlines use to assess the amount of luggage you can take, the 'piece' system and the 'weight' system. The 'piece' system allows you to take a certain amount of luggage items on the plane, while the more common 'weight' system uses the combined weight of all your luggage.

Most flights from the UK to Mexico apply the piece system, which means that adults and children paying 50 per cent or more of the ticket price are allowed to carry on 2 pieces of luggage each up to 158 cm (62 in) in total dimensions (length + height + width) and maximum weight 23 kg (50 lb) each. This is in addition to hand luggage.

Remember that these allowances can vary from country to country – be sure to check with your airline before you leave.

TRAVEL INSURANCE

Annual insurance policies can make economical sense, depending on how often you go abroad. Shop around and ensure you are covered for any extra activities such as scuba diving, horse riding or watersports – and for emergency medical and dental treatment, including flights home if required.

PRACTICAL INFORMATION

During your stay

ARRIVAL
Forma Migratoria de Turista card

All tourists must fill in a Forma Migratoria de Turista (FMT), a free form available at borders, airports, ports, and Mexican embassies and tourist offices. You must show a passport valid for six months from the date of travel. The form is valid for 180 days and it must be carried on your person at all times and handed in at the airport when you leave. There is a departure tax of US$46 to pay at the time of writing.

BEACHES

All Mexican beaches are public property, although in practice it is often difficult to access a beach without walking through a hotel's property.

> **BEACH SAFETY**
> Take heed of local warnings about currents, which can be dangerous, and be aware that watersports equipment may not meet British safety standards. On the beach, coloured flags indicate how safe the water is. Note that they are different from those in Europe. Green or Blue Flags mean the water is calm and safe for swimming. Yellow Flags indicate that swimmers should exercise caution. Red or Black Flags denote dangerous conditions such as strong undertow; swimmers should get out of the water until lifeguards signal an improvement in the sea's condition.

CHILDREN'S ACTIVITIES

Babysitters can usually be arranged at larger hotels, many of which provide day activities for children. See page 101 for further options.

CONSULATES & EMBASSIES

If you are unlucky enough to need the help of the British government, you will have to contact the Consular Section of the British Embassy in

Mexico City or an Honorary Consulate (Cancún is the only office in the Yucatán). A full list of embassy offices is available at its website (ⓦ http://ukinmexico.fco.gov.uk/eng) and details of the Cancún and Mexico City offices are given below:

Cancún ⓐ Honorary Consulate, The Royal Sands, Boulevard Kukulcán Km 13.5, 77500 Cancún ⓣ 998 881 0100

Mexico City ⓐ British Embassy Consular Section, Río Usumacinta 26, Col Cuauhtémoc, 06500 México DF ⓣ 55 5242 8500

CURRENCY

The peso is the Mexican monetary unit, but US dollars are widely accepted. Coins come in denominations of 10, 20 and 50 centavos (cents) and 1, 2, 5, 10 and 20 pesos; notes come in denominations of 20, 50, 100, 200 and 500 pesos. The symbol, $, is the same as for the US dollar, so expect to be confused.

ELECTRICITY

Mexico's electricity system is 120 V/60 Hz, usually using two flat-pin plugs, so bring a socket adaptor if you plan to use electrical equipment from home. Anything you bring with you that operates at a higher rate of 240 V (such as a hairdryer) will need to be dual-voltage. Those that operate on 12 volts with the use of a special adaptor (transformer) will usually cope with dual voltage, but check before travelling.

EMERGENCY NUMBERS
Ambulance ⓣ **065**
Police ⓣ **060**

GETTING AROUND
Driving
Car hire Major international car rental companies have offices in most cities, airports and bus stations, although local companies are

cheaper. Pre-booking is ideal, but be sure that the price includes 15 per cent tax and full insurance (with theft and collision damage waiver). Drivers must have a full driver's licence, be over 21 (or 25) and have a major credit card.

Rules of the road Distances are measured in kilometres, and driving is on the right-hand side of the road. Seat belts are compulsory and speed limits are: 40 kph (25 mph) in cities; 70 kph (43 mph) in rural areas; and 110 kph (68 mph) on motorways. The police are very vigilant about checking your speed.

Roads Yucatán highways are well built, but smaller roads can be uneven. In villages, watch out for speed bumps, which can often be very high, and unmarked. If you are in need of breakdown assistance, the Ángeles Verdes (Green Angels) – English-speaking mechanics who patrol the major highways in bright-green trucks – offer a free service provided by Mexico's Ministry of Tourism (SECTUR). You only have to pay for spare parts, fuel and a discretionary tip. Call their 24-hour hotline (078) or you can contact them through the national tourist assistance in Mexico City (800 903 9200). There are toll roads (*cuotas*), free roads (*libres*) and *super carreteras*, expensive but fast motorways. Drivers are insured against accident or breakdown on *cuotas*.

Petrol Almost every town will have a government-controlled Pemex station. All petrol is unleaded (*sin plomo*) and is priced by the litre.

Parking A white E (*estacionamiento*) on a blue background indicates a car park. A black E in a red circle means parking is permitted. The same E with a diagonal line through it means no parking.

Public transport

Buses Intercity and long-distance buses can vary dramatically in quality and cost – it is best to go for the more luxurious option. Local buses, or *camiones*, are cheap but have pre-set stops. Minibuses, or *colectivos*, are cheaper than taxis and a step up from the crowded buses. Wave one down and tell the driver where you want to go. The fare is established by the government, depending on how far you go. Pay at the end of the journey.

◔ *A pelican at the Sian Ka'an Biosphere*

Taxis Taxis are common and can be economical if you have luggage. Establish if the driver has a meter – if not, confirm a price first.

Ferries These go to Cozumel from Puerto Morelos (car ferry) and Playa del Carmen (passenger only). Ferries also run from Puerto Juárez (passenger only) and Punta Sam (car ferry) to Isla Mujeres. Another ferry leaves for Isla Mujeres from Cancún's Playa Linda several times daily.

HEALTH MATTERS

Chemists Major resorts will have several *farmácias*. Oral rehydration tablets are free of charge at health centres if suffering from diarrhoea.

Health hazards Beware of jellyfish and coral while swimming – if cut or bitten, be sure to bathe and disinfect. Avoid sunstroke when on a long walk or tour – carry oral rehydration salts, sunscreen, hats and bottled water. If visiting high-altitude areas, allow time to acclimatise – tiredness, shortness of breath and headaches are symptoms of altitude sickness.

Water Drink only bottled water, as tap water can often result in an upset stomach. Also, avoid ice in cold drinks and be wary of street food stalls.

Clinics Visitors must rely on either private treatment or go to the local Civil Hospital (*Centro de Salud*) or Red Cross hospital. Check with your hotel, embassy or tourist office for a list of English-speaking doctors.

OPENING HOURS

Shops are usually open between 09.00 and 19.00 or 20.00, and closed for lunch between 14.00 and 16.00. Most shops close on Sundays, although large shopping centres may stay open, particularly in tourist areas and Mexico City. Banks are usually open 09.00–13.30 Mon–Fri, museums 09.00–17.00 Tues–Sun and archaeological sites are open 08.00–17.00 Mon–Fri. Churches are in frequent use, so be aware of potentially disturbing a service.

PERSONAL COMFORT & SAFETY

Crime prevention Although most tourist areas in the Yucatán are relatively safe, it makes sense not to wear expensive jewellery and flaunt

valuable electrical goods. Pickpocketing in crowded areas does occur.
Avoid withdrawing large sums of money from cash dispensers and try
not to take out money or drive late at night.

Lost property If you have anything lost or stolen, you should report
it to the local police in order to claim on your insurance at home. Lost
passports should be reported to your embassy.

Police There are several different types of police in Mexico, from traffic
and tourist police, to police hired to work on contract to banks and
businesses. As a general rule, the police are best avoided, but the federal
traffic police will help those stuck on the highway, and the tourist police
can often speak some English.

POST OFFICES

Most resorts have an *oficina de correos*, where you can buy stamps and
send or receive post. Rates change often, so check first. For airmail, mark
it 'Por Avión' – remember it can take up to three weeks to reach Europe.

TIME DIFFERENCES

The Yucatán is five hours behind GMT, although much of the rest of
Mexico is on Central Standard Time, which is six hours behind GMT.

TELEPHONES

To call Mexico from the UK, dial 00 52 then the city or area code
followed by the seven- or eight-digit local number.

For long-distance calls within the country, dial 01 plus the area
code then the number. For example, the area code for Cancún is 998.
From outside Cancún, you will need to dial 01, then the three-digit
code, followed by the seven-digit number. From within Cancún,
however, omit the codes and dial only the seven-digit number.

To phone the UK, dial 00 44, followed by the area code (minus
the 0) and the number.

TIPPING

Service in smarter restaurants is sometimes included in the bill, but, if not, add on 10 to 15 per cent – preferably in cash. Taxi drivers do not expect tips, but you can round up the fare. Tipping of tour leaders is at your discretion. Hotel room cleaners will always value a tip.

TOURIST INFORMATION OFFICES

The UK Mexico Tourism Board's website has some basic information and travel hints. ☎ 020 7488 9392 ⓦ www.visitmexico.com

Local tourist offices

Cancún ⓐ Avenida Tulum 26 ☎ 998 884 8073
Cozumel ⓐ Avenida Benito Juárez and Avenida 5 ☎ 987 872 0972
Isla Mujeres ⓐ Avenida Rueda Medina, between Morelos and Madero ☎ 998 877 0767
Mérida ⓐ There is a small information booth at the airport. The main office in the centre of the city is at the Palacio de Gobierno (Government Palace), just off the Plaza Grande (Main Square) ☎ 999 924 9290
Mexico City ⓐ Amberes 54, Esq Londres Col. Juárez ☎ 55 533 4700
Playa del Carmen ⓐ Avenida Juárez and Avenida 15 ☎ 984 884 8073

TRAVELLERS WITH DISABILITIES

Visitors with disabilities may find travel around Mexico difficult. There are few wheelchair ramps, and escalators are far more common than lifts. Visits to the country's world-famous archaeological sites may prove particularly trying. That said, if you choose to stay in one location and pick your accommodation carefully, you are likely to find fewer problems. Newer and more expensive hotels and private villas may have excellent adaptations. Cancún has one of the better-equipped airports in the country, with ramps, disabled toilets and wheelchairs available on request. Ask your travel agent for details, or contact a specialist operator such as Accessible Journeys (ⓦ www.disabilitytravel.com) or Access Able (ⓦ www.access-able.com).

ACKNOWLEDGEMENTS

We would like to thank all the photographers, picture libraries and organisations for the loan of the photographs reproduced in this book, to whom copyright in the photograph belongs:
Alamy Images page 39; Dreamstime.com pages 10–11 (Andrew Howard), 26 (Garnham123), 30 (Spanishalex), 32 (Caroline Garcia Aranda), 67 (Tommy Schultz), 82–3 (Rgaf72), 107 (Dangerphoto), 111 (Timothy Kirk); Jane Egginton pages 9, 23, 73, 79, 100, 102–3; Peter Maas/Wikimedia Commons page 29; Photoshot/NHPA page 61; Photoshot/World Pictures pages 53, 71, 81, 86; Pictures Colour Library pages 95, 121; Superstock page 109; Thomas Cook pages 5, 13, 16, 18, 42, 45, 54, 74–5, 77, 85, 93, 97, 105.

Project editor: Thomas Willsher
Layout: Donna Pedley
Proofreader: Karolin Thomas
Indexer: Marie Lorimer

Send your thoughts to
books@thomascook.com

- Found a beach bar, peaceful stretch of sand or must-see sight that we don't feature?

- Like to tip us off about any information that needs a little updating?

- Want to tell us what you love about this handy little guidebook and more importantly how we can make it even handier?

Then here's your chance to tell all! Send us ideas, discoveries and recommendations today and then look out for your valuable input in the next edition of this title.

Email to the above address or write to:
pocket guides Series Editor, Thomas Cook Publishing, PO Box 227, Unit 9, Coningsby Road, Peterborough PE3 8SB, UK.

Useful phrases

English	Spanish	Approx pronunciation
BASICS		
Yes	Sí	*Si*
No	No	*Noh*
Please	Por favor	*Por fabor*
Thank you	Gracias	*Grathias*
Hello	Hola	*Ola*
Goodbye	Adiós	*Adios*
Excuse me	Disculpe	*Diskoolpeh*
Sorry	Perdón	*Pairdohn*
That's okay	De acuerdo	*Dey acwerdo*
I don't speak Spanish	No hablo español	*Noh ablo espanyol*
Do you speak English?	¿Habla usted inglés?	*¿Abla oosteth eengless?*
Good morning	Buenos días	*Bwenos dee-as*
Good afternoon	Buenas tardes	*Bwenas tarrdess*
Good evening	Buenas noches	*Bwenas notchess*
Goodnight	Buenas noches	*Bwenas notchess*
My name is ...	Me llamo ...	*Meh yiamo ...*
NUMBERS		
One	Uno	*Oono*
Two	Dos	*Dos*
Three	Tres	*Tres*
Four	Cuatro	*Cwatro*
Five	Cinco	*Thinco*
Six	Seis	*Seys*
Seven	Siete	*Seeyetey*
Eight	Ocho	*Ocho*
Nine	Nueve	*Nwebeyh*
Ten	Diez	*Deeyeth*
Twenty	Veinte	*Beintey*
Fifty	Cincuenta	*Thincwenta*
One hundred	Cien	*Thien*
SIGNS & NOTICES		
Airport	Aeropuerto	*Aehropwerto*
Rail station	Estación de trenes	*Estathion de trenes*
Platform	Vía	*Via*
Smoking/	Fumadores/	*Foomadores/*
Non-smoking	No fumadores	*No foomadores*
Toilets	Servicios	*Serbitheeos*
Ladies/Gentlemen	Señoras/Caballeros	*Senyoras/Kabayeros*